STRANGE BUT TRUE
STORIES OF
WORLD WAR II

STRANGE BUT TRUE STORIES OF
WORLD WAR II

By

George Sullivan

WALKER AND COMPANY/NEW YORK

Second Walker Edition 1991

First published in the United States of America in 1983 by the Walker Publishing Company, Inc.
Published simultaneously in Canada by Thomas Allen & Son Canada, Limited, Markham, Ontario.
ISBN: 0-8027-6489-4 Trade
　　　0-8027-6490-8 Reinf.

Library of Congress Cataloging in Publication Data

Sullivan, George
　　Strange but true stories of World War II.

　　Bibliography: p.
　　Includes index.
　　Summary: Accounts of eleven bizarre but true incidents during World War II include a secret alliance between the U.S. Navy and the Mafia and Japanese bombing by balloon of our Midwest.
　　1. World War, 1939–1945—Miscellanea—Juvenile literature. [1. World War, 1939–1945—Miscellanea]
I. Title.
D743.7.S87　1983　940.53　82-23730
ISBN 0-8027-6489-4

Book designed by LENA FONG HOR
Printed in the United States of America

10　9　8　7　6　5　4　3　2　1

CONTENTS

INTRODUCTION

WORLD WAR II was the biggest war in history. It killed more people, cost more money, and destroyed more property than any other before or since.

Battles were fought in almost every part of the world—in Europe, Asia, and North Africa. Submarines and surface vessels clashed in the Atlantic and Pacific oceans and in the Mediterranean Sea.

The United States, Great Britain, France, and their partners were known as the "Allies" during World War II. There were approximately 50 Allied nations.

Germany, Italy, and Japan were the Axis nations. They were supported by the Balkan nations of Rumania and Bulgaria.

During the first years of the war, the Axis powers gained the upper hand. The world watched helplessly as German armies overran Poland in 1939. Germany's armies struck again six months later, taking Denmark, which offered no resistance, and then invaded Norway. The British and French rushed troops to Norway, but it was a hopeless cause.

In May 1940, German forces opened an assault on Belgium, Luxembourg, and the Netherlands. Luxembourg fell in one day and the Netherlands in five. Belgium surrendered in 18 days.

German forces then knifed into France. In four days, the French were in hopeless retreat.

With the fall of France, Germany had conquered six countries in three months. Great Britain stood alone in western Europe. Adolf Hitler, the Germans' wartime leader, boasted his armies would soon march into Britain.

But Hitler decided he would tackle Russia first. Earlier, Germany and Russia had been partners. When Germany invaded Russia, the United States and Britain came to look upon Russia as an ally, and

GERMAN TROOPS OVERRAN SIX COUNTRIES IN THE FIRST THREE MONTHS OF WORLD WAR II. *(Neil Katine, Herb Field Art Studio)*

ADOLF HITLER TOOK CONTROL
OF THE GERMAN
GOVERNMENT IN 1933.
*(From the collection of
Ed Stadnicki)*

began shipping enormous quantities of equipment and supplies to the country.

It was at this time—December 1941—that Japanese planes bombed Pearl Harbor, thrusting the United States into the war.

Almost instantly, the American people joined in a united effort to crush the menacing nations. Young men and women by the millions served willingly, if not enthusiastically, in the army, navy, and marine corps.

On the home front, American factories produced an avalanche of war materials. As American men went into the armed services, women took their places in the war plants.

There were shortages in many consumer goods. Certain items were rationed, including meat, butter, sugar, coffee, and gasoline. American families saved copper, brass, aluminum, tin, and other critical metals to donate to the war effort. People bought war bonds.

Many American cities practiced "blackouts." On specified nights, people would douse their lights, to prevent the city from being an easy target in the event of an enemy bombing.

Virtually every American made some contribution to the war effort. The total effect was a tremendous display of power and might.

Some people made profound sacrifices. Indeed, no one can ever assess the terrible costs in human suffering and loss of life.

The stories of some of those who made great and heroic sacrifices are recounted in this book—the secret agents who lived on the brink of discovery and extinction, the bold British submariners who attacked one of Hitler's most formidable weapons, and the Japanese-Americans who fought with such fervor in support of the Allied cause that they were singled out for special recognition by an American president.

These stories also have a bizarre quality about them, something unusual, something strange. But mainly they are about people and the enormous sacrifices they made.

PEARL HARBOR ATTACK ON DECEMBER 7, 1941, THRUST THE UNITED STATES INTO WORLD WAR II. *(U.S. Navy)*

1

MAJOR MARTIN GOES TO WAR

LATE IN 1942, at the time North Africa was being cleared of Axis troops, the Allies decided the first step in the retaking of Europe should be Sicily, a region of Italy separated from the mainland by a narrow strait at its southeastern tip. Someone once said that Sicily looks like a football about ready to be kicked by the Italian boot.

A quick glance at a map of the Mediterranean Sea shows Sicily to be the logical stepping-stone from the North African coast into southern Europe. The northern tip of Tunisia is, in fact, only 95 miles from the Sicilian coast. Because it was such an inviting target, the Allies knew that the Germans and Italians would be expecting the attack and preparing for it.

How, the Allies asked themselves, could they get the enemy to believe the landings were to be made elsewhere?

Lieut. Comdr. Ewen Montagu and his colleagues

at British Naval Intelligence believed they had the answer: Take an anonymous corpse, give him an identity as a British officer, plant phony documents on him indicating a planned Allied landing on Greece and Sardinia, and allow his body to wash ashore on the Spanish coast. Wait for the body to be discovered by the Spanish and the documents to be turned over to the Germans. Then hope that the Germans would believe the documents were genuine and would change their Mediterranean defense plans so the Allies could invade Sicily with minimum losses.

To confuse and mislead the enemy has always been one of the chief goals of warring nations. Virtually every campaign, indeed, every battle, offers evi-

SICILY, OFF ITALY'S SOUTHWESTERN TIP, WAS LOGICAL STEPPING-STONE INTO SOUTHERN EUROPE. *(Neil Katine, Herb Field Art Studio)*

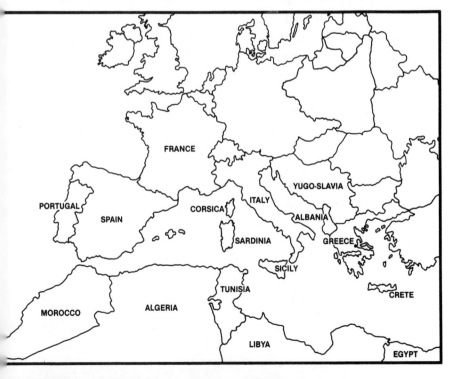

dence of one side's attempt to deceive the other.

The plan involving the anonymous corpse was one of the most preposterous hoaxes of its type hatched during World War II. Yet it was more successful than anyone ever dreamed it would be.

When Comdr. Montagu revealed his scheme for the first time, it immediately raised several questions, such as, where could a body be obtained? That was the most difficult question of all.

Nobody involved in the hoax liked the idea of tinkering with the sanctity of a human body. But the realization that the project could result in the saving of many lives helped overcome their misgivings.

Comdr. Montagu learned of a man in his midthirties who had just died of pneumonia. He sought out the man's relatives and explained as much as he could without giving the secret away. It was a worthwhile cause, he told the relatives, and the man would eventually receive a proper burial. His name would never be revealed. The relatives granted Naval Intelligence permission to use the body.

The corpse was given the name of William Martin and the rank of major in the Royal Marines. An identification card was prepared and the appropriate stamps put on it. Comdr. Montagu didn't want the card to look brand-new so he spent hours rubbing it up and down his trouser leg to age it.

British intelligence experts not only created an identity for the body, but they also made up a personality for it. Letters that the major carried in his pocket gave some idea of what kind of person he was.

A girl friend named Pam was invented for the major. Two letters were handwritten and signed by her. In one, she enclosed a snapshot. The photograph actually depicted a friend of Comdr. Montagu's.

The correspondence that Major Martin carried disclosed that he and Pam were planning to be married and that he had given her an engagement ring. A bill from a jewelry store for the ring was included among the major's papers. A bill from a Naval and Military Club, where he supposedly stayed the night before his ill-fated airplane flight, was also included.

Comdr. Montagu and his fellow conspirators filled Major Martin's pockets with the usual odds and ends a man carries, including several coins, a ring of keys, a pencil stub, a packet of cigarettes, a box of matches, and two theater ticket stubs. A wristwatch was placed on one wrist. A chain with a silver cross and an identification tag was placed around his neck. A wallet was placed in his right back pocket. It contained the photograph of Pam, a book of stamps with two missing, an invitation to the Cabaret Club in London, the identification card, and several pound notes.

Other parts of the plan began to fall into place. It was decided that papers being carried by Major Martin would make it appear that he had floated ashore from an aircraft that had crash-landed at sea.

How should the body fall into enemy hands? Where should it float ashore? Germany itself was ruled out. Comdr. Montagu did not want German doctors examining the body firsthand. Eventually Huelva, Spain, not far from the Portuguese border, was chosen as the landing point for the body. Intelligence officials knew that there was a top-notch German secret agent at Huelva. He would be certain to learn of the body and the documents it carried.

The problem of getting Major Martin into the waters off the Spanish coast had to be solved. The body could not be dropped from an airplane. That would cause injury to it. A ship would be likely to attract attention ashore. Comdr. Montagu and his associates decided that a submarine was the best bet. It could get close to the shoreline without being seen. British naval officials gave the assignment to the submarine *Seraph*.

Major Martin was to be carrying a briefcase that contained several documents. It was to be attached to his body with a leather-covered chain, the type used by some bank messengers when carrying valuable securities. The chain prevented the briefcase from being snatched away from them.

In the case of Major Martin, it was hoped that the Spanish and Germans would believe that the chain served the same purpose. It was actually intended to prevent the briefcase from becoming separated from him.

A great amount of planning went into the preparation of the essential document that Major Martin was to carry in his briefcase, the one that was to give the Germans misleading information. The document took the form of a letter from a very high-ranking officer, Sir Archibald Nye, Vice-Chief of the Imperial Staff, to Sir Harold R. L. Alexander, who commanded an Allied Army in Tunisia under General Eisenhower.

It was a friendly and informal letter from one long-time colleague and friend to another, and was addressed to "My dear Alex" and signed, "Best of luck, Yours ever, Archie Nye."

In the letter Sir Archibald appeared to be turning down certain requests that General Alexander had made for additional troops and supplies. Sir Archibald explained that these men were needed for the assault on Greece, and the letter disclosed that efforts were underway to get the Germans to think that Sicily would be the next target.

A second letter was prepared to explain Major Martin's mission. It was signed by Lord Louis Mountbatten, Chief of Combined Operations, and addressed to Admiral Sir Andrew Cunningham, Commander-in-Chief of Britain's Mediterranean Forces. It declared that Major Martin was a specialist in the use of landing craft and barges, and that his knowledge and experience would be useful in the upcoming invasion. The letter contained references to make the Germans believe that Sardinia, the large island directly south of Tunisia, might be the target for the invasion.

An airtight container was built to hold the body. It looked something like a torpedo with flattened ends. One end was fitted with a lid.

Major Martin was loaded into the sheet metal container. Then it was filled with dry ice. As the dry ice melted into carbon dioxide, it would prevent oxygen from entering the container. This would slow the decomposition of the body.

The container was trucked north to Greenock, not far from where the *Seraph* lay at anchor. A motor launch ferried the container to the submarine. Early in the evening of April 19, 1943, the *Seraph* sailed for Spain.

Comdr. Montagu waited anxiously for news from the submarine. A week went by. Then Naval Intelligence headquarters received a coded message from the *Seraph* reporting that Major Martin had been successfully launched.

Comdr. Montagu later learned that the *Seraph* had surfaced off the Spanish coast not far from the mouth of the Huelva River in the pre-dawn hours of April 23. The steel container was hauled up onto the deck and Major Martin removed from it.

The body was wrapped in a life jacket, assuring that it would float. Officers checked to see that the briefcase was securely attached to Major Martin's wrist.

Major Martin was lowered into the water. Crew members of the *Seraph* then shoved the empty container into the sea and sank it with gunfire. Its task completed, the *Seraph* submerged and moved away.

Not long after, a Spanish fisherman noticed a floating object, which turned out to be the body of Major Martin. The body was brought ashore and military officials were summoned. A Naval officer took charge of the documents and personal effects.

After being examined by a Spanish doctor, who reported Major Martin had drowned, the body was turned over to British diplomatic officials in Huelva. They arranged for a military funeral and for Major Martin's burial in the cemetery there. When Comdr. Montagu learned of this, he arranged for a wreath to be placed on the grave from Pam and the major's family.

At the time the body had been turned over to the British, mention had been made of the briefcase and the documents the major had been carrying. British officials demanded that the Spanish turn them over. Eventually they did.

When the documents finally reached London, Comdr. Montagu examined them. The envelope seals appeared not to have been broken, but scientific tests disclosed that the envelopes had been opened and their contents removed. Comdr. Montagu felt certain that German agents had been permitted to make copies of them.

In the early morning hours of July 10, 1943, the Allies invaded Sicily. The American task force was made up of 580 vessels and 1,124 landing craft. The British task force consisted of 795 ships and 715 landing craft. Despite their enormous size, the task forces suffered only minor losses. One admiral remarked that it was "almost magical that great fleets of ships could remain anchored on the enemy's coast . . . with only such slight losses from an attack as were incurred."

Some 478,000 troops—228,000 American, 250,000 British—landed on the Sicilian beaches in the first three days. The landings met little opposition and the beach defenses were quickly overthrown.

After 39 days, Allied forces occupied all of Sicily. They later were to use the island as a springboard for their invasion of Italy. Mussolini fell from power in Italy during the fighting in Sicily.

It was not until several months after the war had ended that Comdr. Montagu learned how Major Martin had influenced the Sicilian campaign.

Documents found in the German naval archives revealed that their agents had telegraphed the contents of the letters carried by Major Martin to their superiors in Berlin. There the letters were treated with the greatest importance. The translation into German of the letter from Sir Archibald Nye to General Alexander was stamped MOST SECRET and made available to top-level German officials. Even Admiral Karl Doenitz, Commander-in-Chief of the German Navy, had initialed the letter, indicating that he had read it. Hitler learned of the documents from Doenitz.

A report that the Germans circulated with the let-

CLOSE TO HALF A MILLION ALLIED TROOPS LANDED ON SICILIAN BEACHES IN FIRST THREE DAYS OF INVASION. THEY MET LITTLE OPPOSITION. *(National Archives)*

ter stated, "The genuineness of the captured document is above suspicion." Other reports gave evidence that the personal papers that Major Martin carried had been carefully inspected.

The German High Command acted on the belief that Greece and Sardinia were the targets of the Allied invasion. A newly-formed German motorized division was sent to Sardinia to reinforce Italian troops there. Another motorized division was sent across France to Greece.

The German Naval Command ordered the laying of minefields off the Greek coast. A group of German submarines was transferred from Sicilian waters to the Aegean Sea.

Even after the first landings in Sicily, the Germans still could not believe that they had been misled. They thought the Sicilian attack was meant to divert their attention from the real invasions that were to come. A bulletin went out to German agents to be on the lookout for an Allied convoy bound for Sardinia.

The scheme concocted by Comdr. Montagu and his associates fooled the Spanish, who were working with the Germans, fooled German intelligence officers in Spain and Berlin, and fooled the German High Command. The plan even fooled Hitler.

No one knows for sure how many thousands of American and British lives were saved by Comdr. Montagu's hoax, but one thing is certain—Major Martin served the Allies well.

2

THE BOMBING
OF AMERICA

Early on the morning of February 25, 1942, citizens of Los Angeles and surrounding communities were awakened by the clattering sound of antiaircraft fire. For 11 weeks, or ever since the Japanese had bombed Pearl Harbor the previous December, Los Angeles, San Francisco, Portland, Seattle, and other cities of the West Coast had been on military alert. Radar stations reported unidentified aircraft, and nightly blackouts were ordered from the San Joaquin Valley to the Mexican border.

Now, with the cannonading of antiaircraft guns and the wailing of sirens, citizens of Los Angeles were having their worst fears confirmed—Japanese bombs were raining down upon them.

The next day, newspapers reported in banner headlines about the "air raid" that had taken place.

There was, however, no air raid. What had happened that February morning was a by-product of the fear and hysteria that gripped many parts of the West Coast in the early months of World War II. Radar personnel *thought* they had detected enemy planes. Antiaircraft gun crews, who poured more than 1400 shells into the sky that night, *thought* they had heard them.

This is not to say that the mainlands of the United States and Canada were not subjected to aerial bombardment during World War II. Indeed, they were. But when the bombs fell—and they *did* fall—the craft that delivered them were not detected by radar. No antiaircraft fire greeted them. Nor did newspapers report the bombings. The bombing of America was, in fact, one of the best-kept secrets of World War II.

In April 1942, only four months after the attack on Pearl Harbor, American forces stunned the Japanese with a bold assault on their homeland. Thirteen two-engined B-25s, taking off from the deck of the aircraft carrier *Hornet*, dropped 500-pound bombs on Tokyo and on military bases in the area. Three more B-25s, also from the *Hornet*, struck at other Japanese industrial centers.

The attack was so unexpected that it threw the Japanese nation into a state of shock. It was an embarrassment to the Japanese military leaders, who had promised the citizens their home islands would never be attacked.

In the weeks that followed, Japanese leaders sought some dramatic way of striking back. The Japanese knew about a terrible fire that had ravaged northwestern Oregon in the 1930s, laying to waste hundreds of thousands of acres of timberland and

AMERICAN BOMBING RAID OF JAPAN IN 1942, LAUNCHED FROM AIR-
CRAFT CARRIER *HORNET*, MADE JAPANESE MILITARY LEADERS HUNGER
FOR REVENGE. *(U.S. Navy)*

threatening several towns. Japanese military leaders
made plans to trigger similar fires by dropping incendiary bombs. Such fires, they believed, would
cause panic among the American people.

In August 1942, the Imperial Navy ordered one of
its unusual aircraft-carrying submarines into position off the southwestern coast of Oregon. On September 9 of that year, and again on September 29, a
small bombing plane, launched from the deck of the
submarine, made several bombing runs over Oregon's Siskiyou National Forest.

The plane reached its target each time, dropped
two incendiary bombs, and returned to the submarine. But because the woodlands had been soaked

by rain, the bombs did no real damage. Only one of them actually started a fire and it was quickly doused by forest rangers.

By this time, the tide of war in the Pacific had begun to turn against the Japanese. In June 1942, the Battle of Midway had taken place, a great naval victory for the United States. Japanese losses at Midway included four big aircraft carriers and a cruiser.

With their forces now on the defensive, Japanese naval officials decided not to risk their aircraft-carrying submarines in the heavily patroled coastal waters of the United States. But the Japanese did not abandon their plan to bomb the American mainland. They merely began to consider other methods.

During the 1920s, Japanese scientists had begun studying the jet stream, the narrow stream of strong westerly winds located six to twelve miles above the ground. In gathering information about the jet stream, the scientists would send high altitude balloons into the air currents, and then attempt to monitor the flight of these balloons as they drifted across the Pacific Ocean. Sometimes the balloons would travel all the way to the United States before coming to earth.

Japanese scientists learned a great deal about the jet stream from the weather balloons. The country's military experts decided this knowledge could be put to use on behalf of the war effort.

Major General Sueki Kusaba was put in charge of a program to use high altitude balloons to carry bombs to targets in the United States. He quickly lined up the support of the nation's scientists, uni-

COLD AIR

COOL AIR

LOW

COLD FRONT

WARM FRONT

JET STREAM WINDS, BLOWING FROM WEST TO EAST, CARRIED BALLOONS AND THEIR BOMB CARGOES TO THE UNITED STATES AND CANADA. *(National Oceanic and Atmospheric Administration)*

versity professors, and balloon manufacturers.

Out of the development program came two types of balloons, one made of paper, the other of rubberized silk. The paper balloons were manufactured in two sizes. A paper balloon that was 45 feet in diameter was developed for use in the summer months. A smaller balloon, 30 feet in diameter, was designed for winter winds. The balloon of rubberized silk was about the same size as the smaller of the paper balloons. The balloons were to be filled with hydrogen.

The balloons were designed to drift along at altitudes of more than 30,000 feet, where they would

24

be mere specks in the sky. Even on the clearest days, they would be out of range of fighter and interceptor aircraft. Even radar would not be able to detect them.

Five bombs in a cluster were suspended from each balloon. After the balloon had been in the air a sufficient amount of time to reach the United States—about 72 hours, according to most estimates—a timing device would release the bombs, which would explode on impact. Another timing device would trigger an explosion that would destroy the balloon. Thus there would be no evidence to indicate where the bombs had come from.

General Kusaba targeted the balloons on the line that cuts across the heart of America marking the 40th degree of north latitude. Redding, California; Reno and Ely, Nevada; Provo, Utah; and Denver, Colorado, are among the cities that lie close to the line. It also forms the Nebraska-Kansas border. Of course, General Kusaba realized that the balloon bombings would not occur exactly on the line, but north or south of it.

It was not until November 1944 that the Japanese were ready to launch their "windship weapon," as they called it. By this time, the war was going very badly for them. American forces had taken many of Japan's strongholds in the Pacific and had invaded the Japanese-held Philippine Islands. Japan's home islands were under constant attack by America's B-29 bombers.

The bomb-carrying balloons represented the final effort on the part of the Japanese to stave off defeat. Between November 1944 and Japan's surrender on

EACH BALLOON CARRIED CLUSTER OF FIVE BOMBS. THIS IS ONE OF THEM. *(National Archives)*

BALLOON PACKAGE ALSO INCLUDED TIMING DEVICE TO DETONATE BOMBS. *(National Archives)*

August 14, 1945, between 6,000 and 10,000 high altitude balloons, each carrying bombs, were released into the jet stream to be carried to the United States.

When the balloons started arriving, they triggered bewilderment rather than fear. One of the first balloons came down in a clump of trees on a ranch near Yerington, Nevada. The balloon itself was undamaged, but the bombs and the timing devices were missing.

The rancher, believing that the strange object might belong to the military, reported it to the Nevada Naval Ammunition Depot. Nobody there was interested. So the rancher cut up the balloon and made haystack covers out of it. Later, when military experts became aware of what the balloon represented and showed up at the ranch to investigate, they were upset to learn what the man had done.

Another of the first balloons to arrive dropped its bombs near Thermopolis, Wyoming, the night of December 6, 1944. When people heard the explosion, they thought that an American plane had dropped a bomb by mistake. The Thermopolis *Independent-Record* declared: "A bomb so carelessly dropped . . . could have done extensive damage, and even might have hit the town . . ."

Fragments of the bomb were identified as being of Japanese manufacture. American military experts scratched their heads in disbelief. How could a Japanese bomb explode in Wyoming?

Later in December, parts of two damaged balloons were found in Alaska. On December 31, a balloon was found lodged in the top of a tree near Estavada, Oregon. It was salvaged by the Oregon State

Police, who turned it over to military authorities.

Late in the afternoon of January 4, 1945, a tremendous explosion rocked the home of a Medford, Oregon, woman. When she looked out the window she saw that a huge hole had been ripped in the yard not far from her house.

After a telephone call to nearby Camp White, the Army sent scores of soldiers to search the area. Local women spent most of the night making coffee and sandwiches for them. The soldiers recovered bomb fragments, which again were identified as having been manufactured in Japan.

The same day a balloon was recovered near Sebastopol, California, about 55 miles north of San Francisco.

Recovered balloons and their parts were sent to the Naval Research Laboratory at Anacostia, D.C., where scientists examined them. They then issued this report:

> It is now presumable that the Japanese have succeeded in designing a balloon which can be produced in large numbers at low cost and which is capable of reaching the United States and Canada from the Western Pacific carrying incendiaries and other devices. It must be assumed that a considerable number are coming over.

Not long after the report was issued, an American fighter plane shot down a balloon near Alturas, California. The balloon was recovered almost intact with its bombs attached. It was rushed to the Naval Air Station in Sunnyvale, California, for study. There

ONE BALLOON WAS RECOVERED INTACT, REFILLED WITH HELIUM, AND TEST FLOWN. *(National Archives)*

the bullet holes were patched and the balloon was refilled with helium and test flown. Men kept a tight hold on the shroud lines so it would not sail away.

Within a four- or five-week period, military experts obtained evidence of nineteen balloon incidents in five western states, plus Hawaii and Alaska (which were not states at the time) and three Canadian provinces. There could be no doubt now—the American continent was under attack.

Since these bombs fell mostly in rural areas and during the winter and spring when wooded areas were snow-covered or wet from rain, they caused little damage. But wherever a bomb fell, people became jittery.

Although American intelligence experts realized

the Japanese were sending the bombs, they did not know how to stop them. Reports of exploding bombs continued to be received from Oregon, California, and Washington. Towns in Arizona, Colorado, Texas, and Utah also reported being attacked from the sky. Some balloon-bombs even traveled as far into the American heartland as Iowa, Kansas, and Nebraska. The balloon that journeyed the farthest reached Grand Rapids, Michigan.

The most unusual balloon recovery was made near Tremonton, Washington, by Sheriff Warren Hyde. As the balloon drifted down, Sheriff Hyde got a tight hold on the bomb package. A strong gust sent the balloon back into the air with Sheriff Hyde still holding on. He "flew" the balloon for several minutes before it drifted back to the ground again.

Early in May 1945, bombs that landed near.Bly, Oregon, resulted in tragedy. A minister's wife and several of her Sunday-school students, picnicking in the woods on the slope of Gearheart Mountain, came upon a bomb cluster in a forest clearing. Someone went up to the package and started to tamper with it. There was a tremendous explosion. Six members of the picnic party, five of them children, were killed.

Military experts did all they could to keep the balloon bombings a secret. Newspaper and radio stations (there was hardly any television then) were asked to keep silent about what was happening—and they did.

Photographing the balloons was forbidden. One man who snapped a picture of a balloon near Bigelow, Kansas, had his film taken by the Army. Another man photographed bombs that landed near

Hyatt Lake, Oregon. The Army confiscated his film also.

Jerrine May, a young reporter for the *Sentinel* in Goldendale, Washington, learned from the local sheriff's office of a "strange object" that had fallen to earth outside of town. She drove out to see it and found a big balloon with sand bags and metal fittings attached. She photographed everything for her

BOMB "INCIDENTS" HAVE BEEN REPORTED FROM THESE AREAS OF UNITED STATES AND CANADA. *(Neil Katine, Herb Field Art Studio)*

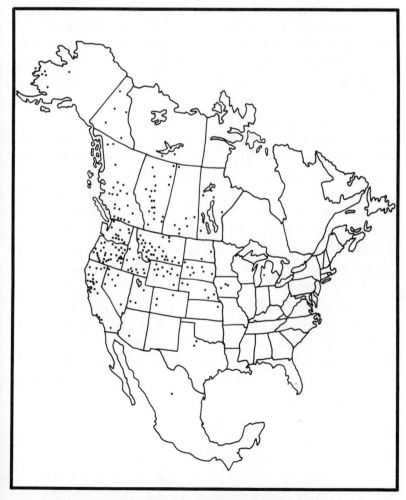

paper. When the Washington State Police found out what she had done, they allowed her to keep her film, but only after she promised not to use the photographs in her paper.

"Nothing ever appeared," Ms. May once said. "A real scoop down the drain. But," she added, "as a souvenir of the night's escapade I did manage to snitch a little piece of the balloon."

As a result of the government-imposed secrecy, the great majority of Americans never knew about the bombings until the war was over.

In addition, the Japanese Military High Command was never able to learn whether the bombs were reaching the United States. They began to question whether the project was worth the time, money, and manpower.

This feeling, plus the fact that factories making balloon parts were being destroyed by American bombing attacks, caused the Japanese to gradually shut down the balloon-bomb program.

Of the many thousands of balloons launched by the Japanese, a total of 329 are known to have fallen on 26 American states and the northern and western provinces of Canada during the war. Several bombs traveled as far south as Mexico. Oregon led all states in bomb incidents with 42.

Since the end of the war, 13 more balloons and their parts have been discovered. It is believed that hundreds more, still with their bomb cargoes, may lie undiscovered in the forests and on the plains of the western half of the United States, a deadly peril to those who might come upon them.

3

OPERATION X-CRAFT

The Time: September 9, 1943.
The Place: The Norwegian island of Spitsbergen on the southern fringe of the Arctic Circle, 400 miles to the north of Norway's northern border.

 Dawn is just breaking. A lookout posted high behind the tiny village of Barentsburg peers into the ocean mists. A small warship, a destroyer, slides through the still water. Then he sees a second ship, the same size as the first, then a third, then several more.

Suddenly the lookout gasps in disbelief. Steaming past is the biggest warship he has ever seen in his life, a great mountain of gray steel, bristling with guns. He knows at once it is the German battleship *Tirpitz*, one of Hitler's mightiest weapons.

The lookout races to a nearby wireless station. Together he and the radio operator count the ships. Besides the *Tirpitz* and the destroyers, there is a second battleship, but even it is dwarfed in size by the giant *Tirpitz*.

The radioman taps out a hurried message to the Allied military post at Reykjavik, Iceland. "Two heavy warships and ten destroyers are approaching Spitsbergen," the message says. It was to be the last word received from the Spitsbergen wireless station.

Hardly had the message been transmitted, when the *Tirpitz* boldly eased its way into Spitsbergen's main inlet from the sea, its biggest guns trained on the first of its targets, the wireless station. For the next several minutes, the sheer rocky walls of the fjord resounded with the thunder of the *Tirpitz*'s powerful guns. Smoke and flame erupted from dozens of different targets. The other ships joined in the bombardment.

Following their carefully developed plan, three of the destroyers, under cover provided by the *Tirpitz*'s hammering blows, tied up at one of Spitsbergen's wharfs and unloaded German assault troops. The Norwegian garrison was small, numbering only 150 men, and while they fought valiantly from their bunkers and foxholes, hitting or wounding many of the invading troops, they were no match for the firepower of the Germans. It was over quickly. Those Norwegians who did not die in the fighting or escape into the bleak hills, were taken prisoner by the German forces.

Then began the systematic destruction of everything on the island that could be of even the slightest value to the Allies. The weather station and the wireless station, vitally important to the Allied convoys as they plowed their way toward Russia, were blown up. The power plant and the waterworks were destroyed by shells from the *Tirpitz* and the other vessels. Huge tanks of fuel and mountains of coal were set afire. Piers and other port facilities were wrecked by demolition crews.

The entire operation took only five hours. By early afternoon, the *Tirpitz* was heading home. Gun crews at the ship's stern could see the smoke from the island's burning ruins for hours. The next morning, when the *Tirpitz* entered the coastal waters of Norway, the Allied wireless station in Iceland was still trying to make contact with Spitsbergen.

The *Tirpitz*'s destination was Kaafjord, Norway, the ship's home port. (Norway had been invaded by the Germans in April 1940, and was now occupied by enemy forces.) But Kaafjord was not a port in the usual sense of the word. It was rather a natural fortress that the Germans, with cleverness and great technical skill, had made secure beyond doubt.

As the *Tirpitz* neared the approaches of Kaafjord, the ship began to follow a zigzag course, picking its way through an extensive minefield that had been laid down by the Germans. The minefield represented the outer line of defense against any Allied ships that might be in pursuit.

Leaving the minefield, the *Tirpitz* passed the fishing village of Hammerfest, the northernmost settlement on the European continent. Just off the coast at Hammerfest, three small islands—Kvalo, Seiland, and Soroy—are clustered together, separated by the narrowest of channels.

As the *Tirpitz* approached the channel, antisubmarine nets guarding the entrance swung open, and the big ship slipped through. Now the *Tirpitz* and its escorting vessels began to ease their way inland through the deep, clear waters of Norway's intricate fjord system. Steep cliffs rose sharply on each side of the channel. In some places, glaciers spilled down to meet the water, which, because of the Gulf Stream, remained ice-free all year round.

Beyond the cliffs was a frozen, treeless land, often battered by snowstorms that lasted for days. German occupation troops stationed there believed it to be the loneliest place in the world.

As the *Tirpitz* made its way inland, there was increasing evidence of the German defense system. The saucer-shaped antennae of radar stations probed the skies for aircraft. For each radar station, there was an antiaircraft battery. Occasionally a patrol of German soldiers could be seen. The Germans had to be constantly vigilant to ward off Norwegian saboteurs.

At the end of the channel there was another anti-submarine net made of steel cables that had been woven into mesh. The net was suspended into the water from buoys at the surface so that it hung in the water like an enormous metal curtain. Shore batteries on either side of the channel guarded the net, which opened to admit the *Tirpitz* and its accompanying vessels and then quickly closed.

The *Tirpitz* had now arrived at its anchorage at Kaafjord, a small cove surrounded by towering fjords on three sides. No sooner did the vessel's engines stop and the mooring lines go out than a heavy steel antitorpedo net was drawn about the *Tirpitz*. Completely ringing the ship, the net protected every square inch of the hull.

While here, the Germans believed the *Tirpitz* to

be absolutely safe. Should Allied dive bombers penetrate the cordon of antiaircraft batteries that pocketed the approaches to Kaafjord, the planes would surely collide with the steep fjord walls as they made their upward turn. Torpedoes from torpedo planes would explode harmlessly on the heavy nets that surrounded the ship.

There were also minefields, shore batteries, antisubmarine nets, and fighter planes. In addition, the Germans had installed smoke screen equipment near where the *Tirpitz* was moored. Should a German radar unit detect approaching enemy planes, Kaafjord could be engulfed in great clouds of dense black smoke that would obscure the precise location of the *Tirpitz* and the other ships.

HEAVILY CAMOUFLAGED, THE *TIRPITZ* LIES AT ANCHOR IN A NORWEGIAN FJORD. *(U.S. Navy)*

The *Tirpitz* had the firepower to challenge any Allied warship afloat, but the Germans had no wish to risk the ship in battle. Although it was used occasionally to lead an assault upon an Allied convoy on its way to Russia, its value lay in its ability to make such raids at will. The British Navy was thus forced to hold two of its biggest battleships in constant readiness for convoy duty. The American Navy also contributed ships for the purpose of checkmating the *Tirpitz*.

The British had been trying to sink the *Tirpitz* almost from the day the ship had completed its sea trials early in 1942. When the *Tirpitz* was anchored in the Trondheim fjord on Norway's west coast, the Royal Air Force had made several attacks upon it, but scored no hits.

The bombing raids would have continued had the *Tirpitz* not moved north to Kaafjord, where it was beyond range of British land-based bombers, another reason the site had been selected as a haven.

British naval experts agreed that the only way in which the *Tirpitz* might be successfully attacked was by submarine. It would have to be a submarine of a special type, one light enough to float right over the minefields at high tide. It would have to be fitted with tools and equipment to cut through the submarine nets, and it would have to be large enough to carry sufficient explosives to rip a hole in the armored hull of the *Tirpitz*—a hole big enough to sink or cripple it.

Early in 1942, the British began testing such a vessel, a midget submarine. They called it an X-craft. Forty-eight feet long, it had the cigar shape of a standard submarine, but it was only 5 1/2 feet in diameter. A man inside could not stand erect; he could only crouch, sit, squat, or lay down.

By May 1942, the tests were completed and the British Navy ordered six of the X-craft, each to be manned by a crew of four. In January 1943 the six vessels were delivered to Loch Cairnbawn in Scotland, some 1,200 miles from Kaafjord and the *Tirpitz*.

Now the Royal Navy had to solve the problem of getting the X-craft within striking distance of the target. The long journey under their own power would take two weeks, too long for crew members to spend in such cramped quarters. They would arrive tired and aching, unfit to carry out their mission. Carrying the subs on a deck of a freighter or other surface ship was too risky.

After weeks of experimentation, the Navy devised a solution. The midget subs would be towed underwater by submarines to the target area.

Instead of torpedoes, each of the midget subs was to be armed with two huge explosive charges, each weighing two tons. Sturdy clamps held the charges in place, one on each side of the X-craft's hull.

The plan was for each X-craft to plant its charges beneath the hull of the *Tirpitz* or one of the other warships. Timing devices controlled from inside the X-craft, similar to the workings of an alarm clock, could be set to go off after an interval long enough to permit the X-craft to escape.

Through the spring and summer of 1943, while the submarines were tested and retested, British Intelligence was gathering information about the *Tir-*

pitz and her sister ships. Agents took aerial photographs of the net defenses and detection systems. Members of the Norwegian resistance movement, linked to agents in England by secret radio, furnished daily reports about the *Tirpitz* and its activities based on information provided by Norwegians who supplied the *Tirpitz* with food and other provisions, by chauffeurs and taxi drivers, and by Kaafjord fishermen.

On September 11, 1943, just one day after the *Tirpitz* had returned to Kaafjord after its pulverizing raid on Spitsbergen, the six X-craft and their towing submarines left Loch Cairnbawn on what was to be one of the most incredible missions of World War II.

The towing operation was filled with hazards. The towlines for the X-8 and X-9 snapped before the vessels reached the Norwegian coast, and both submarines—and three of the crew members—were lost as a result. On September 20, the four remaining X-craft were in position off Kaafjord ready to launch the attack.

Lt. Donald Cameron, a 26-year-old Scotsman, was in command of one of the midget submarines, the X-6. He and his crew were to play a major role in events of the next few days.

Not long after dark the X-6 was released from its towing submarine, running on the surface to conserve fuel and charge its batteries. Shortly after midnight it approached the minefield protecting the entrance to the inland waterway leading to Kaafjord. Cameron moved his craft as close to shore as he safely could. He knew there were no mines here because they would disrupt offshore boat traffic. By

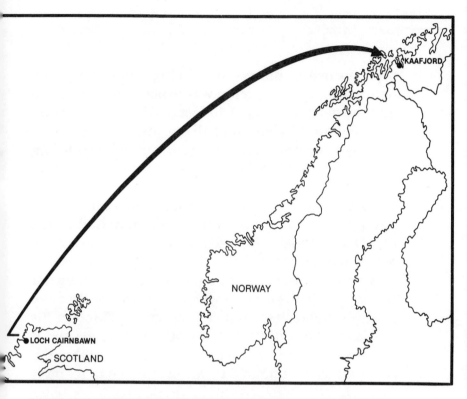

ROUTE OF X-CRAFT FROM LOCH CAIRNBAWN, SCOTLAND, TO KAAFJORD, NORWAY. *(Neil Katine, Herb Field Art Studio)*

keeping close to the shoreline, he knew he could skirt the first of the antisubmarine nets, which guarded only the deepest waters of the channel.

By the next morning, the X-6 was running in enemy waters about four miles from where the *Tirpitz* was moored. Through the periscope, Cameron scouted German antiaircraft emplacements. Occasionally a patrol boat went chugging by. That night they ran on the surface again.

Cameron realized that the woven net of steel that guarded the entrance to Kaafjord was to be the sternest test the X-6 would face. His crew had a plan for conquering the net. Don Kendall, one of the four, had been trained in underwater diving and the use of a net-cutting gun. Cameron was to nose the submarine into the net at a depth of 40 feet and keep pressure on the steel mesh while Kendall cut away.

It was tricky business. Getting Kendall into the water and back on board again was hazardous in itself. The procedure called for Kendall to enter the sub's escape chamber, flood it, open the escape hatch, and then climb over the slippery hull to the net. Once he had completed his work, he would have to reverse the procedure.

Cameron was bringing the X-6 into position for the net cutting operation when he heard the drone of a ship's propellers passing over them. Through his periscope, he could see it was a fishing boat, and it was heading straight for the net. This meant that the net had been opened to allow the boat to pass through.

"We might be able to go through behind her," Cameron said to a crewman, but he knew that underwater the engine of the X-6 could not propel them through the water fast enough to keep pace with the fishing boat. The net would close before they reached it. When the X-6 was on the surface, its engine was powerful enough to do the job.

"Surface!" ordered Cameron. "Full speed ahead."

When the fishing boat passed through the open gate, the X-6 was right behind. Not a soul, either aboard the boat or on shore, noticed.

Once in the cove at Kaafjord, Cameron took the X-6 to periscope depth. As he scanned the surface, he could see German warships of every size. A tanker was anchored about two miles away. Two destroyers were moored to the tanker, refueling. Just beyond lay the *Tirpitz*. Cameron's heart pounded.

Only one obstacle now stood between the X-6 and the succesful completion of its mission—the anti-torpedo nets that surrounded the *Tirpitz*. According to British Intelligence, the nets extended from the surface to a depth of 50 feet. The plan called for the X-craft to pass *under* the nets.

Cameron took the X-6 to 80 feet. They rammed into the net. At 100 feet, the same thing happened. Upon inspection, Cameron learned the nets extended all the way to the bottom. British Intelligence had been wrong.

The men aboard the X-6 were stunned. They had come so far; they had gotten so close. Were they now forced to turn back without accomplishing their mission?

Cameron took the X-6 to periscope depth. He noticed that there was an opening in the ring of steel mesh that surrounded the *Tirpitz*. A sliding metal barrier filled the opening. It was a gate for small boats.

Off to one side, Cameron spotted a small motor launch approaching the gate. "We did it once," he thought to himself. "We might be able to do it again.

"Surface depth," Cameron declared. Then he ordered the helmsman to follow the motor launch as it passed through the gate. As soon as they were inside, Cameron cried out, "Dive! Dive!"

It was not long after seven o'clock in the morning and the sun was shining brightly. A lookout aboard the *Tirpitz* saw what he described as a "long black thing" pop up out of the water and then disappear again. "It looked like a submarine," he reported to the deck officer.

But no one in authority aboard the *Tirpitz* could believe that a submarine had actually penetrated the defense system. "Perhaps it was a dolphin," one officer said. "Perhaps it was a log," said another. When the report reached the captain that a suspicious object had been sighted in the water, he ordered an emergency alarm to be sounded. "It's better to be on the safe side," he said. By that time, 13 minutes had passed.

Below the surface, Cameron swung the X-6 under the keel of the *Tirpitz*. He set the charges to go off in one hour and then ordered the men to release them. The two big bombs fell away from the X-6 and came to rest in the thick mud below the bottom of the *Tripitz*'s hull.

Cameron knew there could be no escape for him and his crew. Even if they had not already been sighted, the X-6 would surely be seen when they tried to go back through the net gate. Destroyers just outside would pounce on them.

Cameron informed his men that they had no choice but to take the X-6 to the surface and surrender. Since they did not want to have the Germans capture the craft, they planned to open up the seacocks, letting the water flood in, and send the X-6 to the bottom.

Cameron ordered all maps, charts, and secret documents to be destroyed. Secret material, he realized, could lead the Germans to the other submarines involved in the mission.

After the documents had been destroyed, Came-

CREW MEMBERS POSE WITH THEIR X-CRAFT. *(Imperial War Museum, London)*

ron said, "We'll surface now and open the seacocks."
The X-6 rose slowly. The crew members of the *Tirpitz* peppered the craft with bullets.

Ed Goddard, the engineman aboard the X-6, volunteered to go out first. When he swung the hatch open, the rifle fire stopped. Goddard climbed out, his hands high above his head. The others followed.

A motor launch from the *Tirpitz* pulled alongside and Cameron and the other crewmen were ordered to jump aboard. As the motor launch swung about and headed for the *Tirpitz*, the X-6 slipped quietly beneath the surface. Forty-five minutes remained before the charges were to explode.

Once aboard the *Tirpitz*, the men from the X-6 were told they could not communicate with one another. Each man was carefully searched.

At about eight o'clock, only minutes before the bombs were set to explode, Cameron and one of the other crewmen were taken to separate cabins for questioning. The two other men from the X-6 remained on deck, closely guarded.

The seconds ticked away. Not long after eight o'clock, the *Tirpitz* was rocked by two tremendous explosions, one right after the other. The huge vessel was lifted several feet out of the water and then, as it dropped back, it quivered from stem to stern like a steel saw blade. Decks buckled, lights went out, steam hissed from broken valves and pipes, and sailors were thrown about like playthings.

A hole large enough to accommodate a big truck had been blown in the hull of the *Tirpitz*. While the ship did not sink, it never recovered from the blow.

The Germans tried valiantly to get the *Tirpitz* back into service. More than a thousand shipyard workers were sent from Germany to Kaafjord to work on the stricken vessel. After they had toiled for more than eight weeks, German naval officials were forced to announce that the *Tirpitz* would be out of action for many more months.

Early in 1944, the *Tirpitz* steamed slowly and shakily out of Kaafjord to an anchorage farther to the south. In November British bombing planes scored several direct hits. The huge vessel rolled over, revealing an enormous hole in its hull that had been filled with tons of concrete, the wound inflicted by the X-6. The ship that had been such a great source of pride to Hitler and had caused the Allies so much anxiety had been sent to the bottom without firing a

INSIGNE WORN BY X-CRAFT OF-
FICERS AND CREW MEMBERS.
(Imperial War Museum)

shot in battle.

Besides the X-6, the X-7 was the only other of the X-crafts to weave its way through the Kaafjord defenses. The vessel had been sighted by *Tirpitz* crew members and sent to the bottom by depth charges. The captain of the X-7 and one member of the crew, however, managed to escape. The X-5 was unable to penetrate the antisubmarine nets. The X-10 was forced out of the running by mechanical problems.

Cameron and the other crewmen of the X-6, and the two surviving men from the X-7, were removed from the *Tirpitz* on the day after the bombs had exploded, put aboard a small ship, and taken south. They eventually reached a prison camp in northern Germany and remained there until the end of the war.

When Cameron and his colleagues finally returned to England, they were given a triumphant welcome. In official recognition of their mission, the Royal Navy hailed them as "gallant gentlemen, whose daring attack will surely go down in history as one of the most courageous of all time."

47

4

THE BATTLE
OF THE PIPS

 IN MID-MAY 1942, a huge invasion force of 200 ships, including eight aircraft carriers, left the home islands of Japan. The vessels were supported by 600 aircraft.

The Japanese ships and the men they carried had two objectives: to capture Midway Island, about 1,000 miles to the northwest of Hawaii, and to occupy the Aleutians, the long string of rocky, barren islands that extend south and west of Alaska.

In a two-day battle off Midway, the bulk of the Japanese fleet was severely mauled by American planes and suffered the loss of four aircraft carriers and a major part of its aircraft. No troops were put ashore. Experts say that Midway was the turning point that spelled Japan's ultimate defeat.

The Japanese, however, did accomplish their goal in the Aleutian Islands. On June 7, a small force of Japanese landed and captured two of the Aleutians, Kiska and Attu.

The islands were of little strategic value. Usually covered by fog or battered by storms, they were virtually unusable as air or naval bases. But the Japanese occupation of the Aleutians had psychological value. It alarmed Alaskans and Americans living in the Pacific Northwest. They felt the islands could serve as a launching point for further expansion. And Americans everywhere were indignant that the Japanese should be holding American territorial land. (Alaska entered the union in 1959.)

Almost a year later, on May 11, 1943, Americans landed a division of troops on Attu, which defeated the Japanese garrison after about two weeks of intense fighting. The Americans then turned their attention to Kiska. D-Day for the invasion was set for August 15.

During July two powerful task groups of American ships were assigned to waters south of Kiska. Their mission was to bombard enemy installations and destroy enemy vessels seeking to reinforce the island. One group of American vessels consisted of the battleships *New Mexico* and *Mississippi*, plus a pair of destroyers and a minesweeper. The second group boasted four heavy cruisers, the *Wichita*, *Louisville*, *Portland*, and *San Francisco*, the light cruiser *Santa Fe*, and a protecting screen of five destroyers. Rear Admiral Robert C. Griffen was in charge of both groups.

Toward the end of July Admiral Giffen received the news that the Japanese Fifth Fleet—two heavy cruisers, two light cruisers, and several destroyers—had left its home base in the Kuriles, the chain of small islands off the northeast coast of Asia that extends north from Japan. The Fleet's destination was not known. However, a shore-based navy scout plane had reported a radar contact with several unidentified objects on the ocean's surface about 315 miles southwest of Kiska. Were they the Japanese ships? Nobody knew for certain.

Foul weather hampered efforts to establish contact with whatever ships might be in the area. Most days were shrouded with heavy fog. Lookouts on the ships could make out only the gray bulk of the ship dead ahead.

Not long after midnight on July 26, the two American naval groups were steaming about 80 miles south of Kiska. A layer of thick clouds blotted out all but a few stars. Suddenly the radar operator aboard the *Mississippi* spotted several "pips," or bright dots of light, on the radar screen he was monitoring. The pips appeared to be a cluster of large ships about 15 miles away. Similar reports began to come from the *New Mexico*, *Portland*, and *Wichita*.

Admiral Giffen wasted no time ordering the ships to general quarters. Sailors, roused from their sleep, hurriedly dressed and raced to their battle stations. Battleship guns were trained on the distant targets. Destroyers got into position to launch their torpedoes. Every ship set course for the enemy vessels.

The *New Mexico*'s radar reported six pips. Other ships were less definite, but indicated several. The enemy ships were speeding along at 16 knots and appeared to be heading for Kiska Harbor.

It *must* be the Japanese Fifth Fleet, thought Admiral Giffen. "Commence firing," he ordered. Gun flashes from the *Wichita* and the *Portland* were the

SHIPS OF ALEUTIAN ISLANDS INVASION FLEET ASSEMBLE AT ADAK HARBOR. *(National Archives)*

first to light the nighttime sky. Minutes later the *New Mexico* and *Mississippi* joined in the cannonading.

Several ships, however, stood grim and silent. Radar operators aboard the *San Francisco* and *Santa Fe* were unable to establish contact with the enemy ships. Their gunnery officers cursed the uncooperative radar equipment.

Admiral Giffen believed the Japanese ships were equipped with highly destructive "long lance" torpedoes, and he had no wish to get within range of them. So he kept his vessels three or four miles away, depending solely on radar to keep track of the vessels.

51

The firing continued for half an hour. Oddly, the vessels under attack were silent. No return fire could be heard. No gun flashes could be seen. No enemy searchlights pierced the blackness.

The cruiser *Portland*, in an effort to actually see the enemy ships, fired a few starshells. They brightened several square miles of ocean as they hung in the black sky, but revealed not a single ship.

The destroyers, now poised to launch their torpedoes, kept reporting they were unable to spot anything.

Then, as mysteriously as they had appeared, the radar pips vanished from the radar screens of the *Mississippi*, *New Mexico*, and the other vessels. The puzzled Admiral Giffen ordered the firing to cease.

The two groups of ships steamed toward the area where the pips were believed to have originated. Four hours were spent in a careful search. No trace of the enemy was found—no oil, no debris, no survivors.

The following day an air search of the area could find no evidence of the enemy ships either. The Navy had fired 518 14-inch shells and 487 8-inch shells needlessly.

An investigation followed. According to one answer to the puzzle, the radar pips may have been caused by enemy submarines that dived when the shelling began. Another stated that whales may have been the reason for the radar contact. A third explanation blamed abnormal atmospheric conditions, known in the past to have made radar behave freakishly.

The American ships continued to bombard Kiska.

When the shelling was over, some 34,000 troops were put ashore. They spent five days searching the island until they were convinced it was empty. The Japanese garrison had secretly evacuated Kiska more than two weeks before. Like "The Battle of the Pips," the invasion of Kiska was a great victory, lacking only one element—an enemy!

5

THE MAFIA CONNECTION

I<small>N THE EARLY MONTHS</small> of World War II, the United States faced a disaster that loomed as serious as that of Pearl Harbor. The calamity was not developing in the vast stretches of the Pacific Ocean, but in the Atlantic, where marauding German U-boats were proving fatal to Allied shipping.

In February 1942, German submarines sank nearly 500,000 tons of Allied shipping. In March, the figure jumped to *over* 500,000 tons. In April it dropped to 430,000 tons, but in May the total reached 600,000 tons, and in June, sinkings reached 700,000 tons.

Castastrophe also struck the *Normandie*, the huge transatlantic liner operated by the French. Scheduled to become a troop transport, the *Normandie* caught fire at its pier in New York early in February 1942. As firemen poured water on the burning vessel, it listed heavily to one side, then rolled over.

The *Normandie* never sailed again.

Since the great bulk of ships heading for Europe sailed from New York, port operations there came under close scrutiny. Was information about ship movements being leaked to German submarine commanders? How were German submarines able to refuel and get supplies without returning to their bases in Europe? Who or what might be aiding the U-boats?

Naval intelligence officials in New York began seeking answers to these questions from all possible sources. Lieutenant Commander Charles Heffenden, one of the Navy's most imaginative intelligence officers, suggested that even leaders of the underworld might be called upon. And when he made this suggestion at a meeting in the office of the New York District Attorney, someone suggested the name of Joseph "Socks" Lanza.

JOSEPH "SOCKS" LANZA AT THE TIME OF HIS ARREST IN NEW YORK IN 1942. *(Federal Bureau of Investigation)*

Anyone who knew anything at all about the New York waterfront in the 1940s knew about Socks Lanza. Born and raised on the Lower East Side of New York, the oldest of nine children, he had gone to work on the docks at 16. Hard work and hard brawling had brought him to a dominant position in the United Seafood Workers Union by the time he was 35.

Along the way Lanza had compiled a lengthy police record. At 17 he was arrested for stealing two barrels of copper tubing. At 19 he was accused of breaking and entering. At 25 he was arrested on a murder charge. There were no witnesses and he was released.

At the time Lanza came to the attention of Naval Intelligence, he was in serious trouble. The charge this time was extortion. He was due to face trial for demanding kickbacks from waterfront workers and having them beaten when they refused. One parole officer described him as a "ruthless racketeer."

None of this bothered Naval intelligence officers too much. A lawyer from the District Attorney's office got in touch with Lanza's lawyer. Would Lanza, because of his experience and the contacts he had, be willing to cooperate with the Navy? It was made clear that Lanza would be cooperating purely as a patriotic service; there were no other considerations involved.

When the question was put to Lanza himself, he quickly agreed to cooperate. "I'll go along 100 percent," he said.

The next step was to arrange a meeting between Lanza and Commander Heffenden. The Navy-Mafia partnership was about to be formed. No one had the slightest idea where it was going to lead.

Heffenden was eager to establish whether German submarines were being refueled or resupplied in the coastal waters of the United States. He asked Lanza to start asking questions.

The next day Lanza got down to business. He met with Ben Espy, one of his closest associates, at the ground floor bar of Meyer's Hotel, Lanza's headquarters in the Fulton Fish Market area. Lanza told Espy that he had agreed to cooperate with Naval intelligence officials and he asked Espy to help. Espy said he would.

MEYER'S HOTEL, LANZA'S HEADQUARTERS IN THE FULTON FISH MARKET DISTRICT OF NEW YORK. (*George Sullivan*)

The two men began visiting stores and businesses in the Fish Market area. They asked owners such questions as, "Have you filled any unusually large orders lately?" "Have you noticed unusual activity of any type?"

Lanza and Espy visited the docks where the fishing boats tied up. Lanza was able to talk to the crewmen easily and naturally, as if he were one of them. He asked them, "What's going on out there?" "Have you seen anything?" "Have you seen any evidence of submarines?" The word was passed to hundreds of fishermen that any sign of suspicious activity should be reported to Lanza.

Through Lanza, Heffenden was able to place agents as workers in the market stalls and on fishing boats as crew members. The boats ranged as far north as Maine and as far south as the Carolinas, with the agents scanning the sea for submarine activity.

While the task of "buttoning up" the port of New York seemed to be moving along well, Lanza admitted that he was limited in what he could accomplish. He lacked influence outside the Fish Market and the adjacent docks. For instance, along the Hudson River, where the biggest ships that made up the Atlantic convoys docked, Lanza was getting nowhere. The same situation prevailed on the Brooklyn piers. Lanza had few friends in Brooklyn.

But Lanza suggested a solution—Mafia leader Charles (Lucky) Luciano. He could "snap the whip on the entire underworld," Lanza said.

The 48-year-old Luciano was a well-known figure. By reputation he was one of the master criminals of the day, known to be wily, greedy, and savagely cruel. One crime reporter of the 1930s said of him, "Like some deadly King Cobra, this droopy-eyed thug coiled himself about the Eastern underworld and squeezed it of its tainted gold."

In recent years, however, Luciano's activities had been muzzled. He was serving a prison term of 30 years and had completed only about seven years of the sentence.

Commander Heffenden realized that Socks Lanza had done as much as he could. A total of 49 merchant ships were sunk in April, 1942. The number ballooned to 102 in May. Thousands of crewmen died. Heffenden agreed it would be a good idea at least to talk to Lucky Luciano.

Preparations for the meeting began. Luciano was serving his sentence at Clinton State Prison at Dannemora, near the village of Malone in upstate New York. Cold, bleak, and isolated, Dannemora was known as the Siberia of American prisons.

For the convenience of those who were to visit Luciano in an attempt to win his cooperation, he was moved to Great Meadow Prison at Comstock, New York, not far from Albany. Luciano wasn't told why he was being transferred. But he didn't care. He was happy to be out of Dannemora.

Other events about to take place would make the Mafia leader even happier. Moses Polakoff, Luciano's lawyer, convinced Heffenden and other Naval intelligence officers that the man who had the best chance of persuading Luciano to cooperate was a former close associate of his, Meyer Lansky.

If Luciano was the king of the underworld in the

1940s, Lansky was the prince. Jukeboxes were his domain. He supervised their manufacture, sale, and distribution. Part of every dollar collected from them went to Lansky. Although he had been arrested six times, including once for murder and three times for assaults, Lansky had only one conviction on his record and it was for a minor offense.

In May 1942, the meeting was arranged at Great Meadow Prison. Luciano was not told who his visitors were, and when he was brought into the room where Lansky and Polakoff were seated, he cried out in delight.

For the next half hour, Lansky and Polakoff sought to convince Luciano that he should cooperate with Naval Intelligence in the war effort. Prison officials had made it clear that no "deal" could be made, that the length of Luciano's sentence would not be affected, whether he cooperated or not.

But one thing that Lansky and Polakoff could offer was the promise of frequent and confidential visits from his associates. And, as they pointed out, no one expected Luciano to discuss *only* Naval intelligence matters during such visits.

It was not easy convincing Luciano that he should work with the Navy. There was a problem. The court that had sentenced him had ordered that he be sent back to Italy once he had served his time in prison. If Luciano cooperated with the United States government he would be helping to bring about Italy's defeat. When he returned to Italy, he would fear for his life.

"I want it kept private, kept secret," Luciano told Polakoff. "When I get back to Italy, I don't want to be

CHARLES "LUCKY" LUCIANO COULD "SNAP THE WHIP ON THE ENTIRE UNDERWORLD," IT WAS SAID. *(United Press International)*

a marked man."

Polakoff promised Luciano a guarantee of secrecy.

Then Lansky and Polakoff explained that Joe Lanza had been cooperating with Naval Intelligence and needed help. "Have Lanza come and see me," Luciano said.

When they met, Luciano told Lanza, "Joe, you go ahead. I will get the word out. Everything will go smoothly."

He instructed Lanza to get in touch with Joe Adonis and Frank Costello, other Mafia leaders of the day. "Go and see Frank, and let Frank help along," said Luciano. "This is a good cause." Lanza

MEYER LANSKY, A KINGPIN OF THE NEW YORK UNDERWORLD, AND A CLOSE ASSOCIATE OF LUCIANO'S. *(Federal Bureau of Investigation)*

offered to return to Great Meadow and report on how things were working out. "All right, fine," said Luciano.

Lansky was drawn into the operation, too. He had several meetings with Heffenden and was given a code number as a Naval intelligence contact. In the weeks that followed, Lansky lined up the support of longshoremen and their leaders along the water-front.

There is no doubt that the Navy's Mafia connection produced results. Through the final months of 1942 and into 1943, supplies were shipped from the port of New York in an uninterrupted flow. There was no sabotage. There was no labor unrest. There were no stoppages of any kind. There were not even delays.

Longshoremen, truck drivers, and shippers quit talking about the types of supplies going aboard ships. Everyone who worked on the docks was made to realize that enemy agents were seeking that type of information.

During the war years the alliance of American intelligence agents and Mafia leaders was a well-kept secret. It might have remained so for decades had not Governor Thomas E. Dewey of New York, on January 3, 1946, granted Luciano his release from prison for the purpose of deporting him to his native Italy.

In a statement released to the press at the time, Dewey said: "Upon the entry of the United States into the war, Luciano's aid was sought by the Armed

JOE ADONIS IN A PHOTOGRAPH TAKEN IN 1956. *(Federal Bureau of Investigation)*

Services in inducing others to provide information concerning possible enemy attack. It appears that he cooperated in such effort . . ."

Dewey's statement triggered many questions. Had the Mafia chieftain actually cooperated with the armed services during the war? And if so, what services had he rendered?

In the years that followed, rumor piled upon rumor. Finally, in 1954, Dewey ordered an official investigation of the matter, which established proof of the cooperation between Naval Intelligence and Mafia leaders of the 1940s.

When the report was made public, it raised still another question, a moral question. Was it right for forces of law and order to work hand-in-glove with known criminal leaders?

Winston Churchill may have provided the answer when he once said, "If by some stroke of fate the Devil came out in opposition to Adolf Hitler, I should not feel constrained . . . to make favorable reference to the Devil in the House of Commons."

6

INDIAN WAR CALL

 IN JUNE 1944, American Marines stormed ashore on Saipan, one of the Mariana Islands, determined to take it back from the Japanese. The fighting was intense.

One battalion pressed inland and captured a position that had been vacated by the enemy. No sooner had the Marines begun to dig in and fortify the position than they came under artillery fire. But it was American artillery pounding them, not Japanese.

The men frantically radioed headquarters, explaining their desperate situation. But the Japanese had successfully imitated American voices many times before in such situations, and headquarters personnel believed it was happening again. The shelling continued.

The men protested again. In response, they heard a tense voice from headquarters say, "Do you have a Navajo?"

There *was* a Navajo in their battalion. He picked

up the microphone and spoke a few words in his native tongue to a Navajo at headquarters. Within minutes the artillery fire stopped. The men in the battallion had been saved by the Navajo message.

Many tales of valor and patriotism came out of World War II. One of the most unusual is the story of the Navajo code talkers, young men from the mesas and canyons of Arizona and New Mexico who played a critical role in such Pacific combat arenas as Guadalcanal, Saipan, Tinian, Tarawa, and Iwo Jima.

The Navajo Indians are the largest Indian tribe in the United States. About 100,000 of the tribe's 140,000 members live on the Navajo reservation, which covers parts of Arizona, New Mexico, and Utah.

World War II was an important turning point in Navajo history. Many members of the tribe left the reservation for the first time to serve in the armed forces and work in war-related industries.

The story of the code talkers begins in February 1942 when Philip Johnston, the son of a Protestant missionary to the Navajos, suggested to the Marine Corps the idea of using the Navajo language for sending messages in battle. Johnston was an engineer with the city of Los Angeles at the time, but he had been brought up on the reservation and learned Navajo from his playmates.

Johnston knew that the language was extremely complicated in form and structure. Its unusual rhythms and strange sounds could even baffle language experts. Said one: "It resembles the prayer call of a Tibetan monk mixed with fast American

double-talk and the sound of a hot water bottle being emptied."

The Marine Corps received Johnston's suggestion with skepticism, but agreed to a demonstration of the idea. It was staged at Camp Elliot, near San Diego. Johnston and several young Navajo transmitted by radio, then quickly translated back into English again.

General Clayton B. Vogel, the Camp Commander, watched in amazement. He was quick to realize that the use of Navajo could save invaluable time during battle, since messages would not have to be put into code and then decoded at the receiving end. He also knew that the Navajo language would be a real puzzle to Japanese intelligence experts, who had shown considerable skill in decoding American messages. General Vogel asked for and received permission to develop a code-talker program.

In April 1942, Marine recruiters traveled to Navajo communities in Arizona and New Mexico to select the first code talkers. Twenty-nine young men signed up. They were sent to Camp Elliot for training. Philip Johnston, who entered the Marine Corps in the fall of 1942, was put in charge of the training program.

Johnston and the Navajo volunteers faced a difficult problem. Their language contained no words for many terms that were commonly used in the Marine Corps. There was, for example, no way to say "hand grenade" or "mortar fire." Nor did such words as "battleship" and "submarine" have counterparts in the Indian tongue.

Johnston and his men found Navajo words that

were associated with the military terms they signified. Thus, the code word for observation plane became "ne-as-jah," the Navajo word for "owl." The code word for submarine became "besh-lo," Navajo for "iron fish." Aircraft carrier became "tsidi-ney-ye-hi," for "bird-carrier." The code word for grenade was the Navajo word for potato. Bomb became the word for egg.

The names of birds differentiated types of aircraft, and the names of fish were used for different types of ships. Navajo clan names were given to different Marine Corps units.

An alphabet system was developed to spell proper names and other terms for which no Navajo word was available. The letter "a" was "wol-la-chee," the Navajo word for ant; "b" was "shush," the word for bear, and so on.

Suppose a code talker wanted to transmit the word Saipan. He would spell it out by transmitting these words:

dibeh—Sheep
wol-la-chee—Ant
tkin—Ice
bi-sodih—Pig
wol-la-chee—Ant
nesh-chee—Nut

When the word system was perfected, a code talker was assigned to transmit a message in Navajo to a group of Marine Intelligence officers. The officers were to try to understand the message. They recorded it on tape and took the tape back to their offices to study it. They spent weeks listening to it over and over, but they were never able to make sense out of it.

After the original group of 29 Navajos completed training, 27 were sent to Guadalcanal in the Solomon Islands to begin use of the code in combat. The other two remained in the United States to work as recruiters and instructors. Approximately 450 young Navajos eventually became code talkers.

The radio sets used by the Navajos weighed about 80 pounds and were hard to lug around. Each consisted of a receiver and a transmitter. The set was powered by a generator that had to be cranked by hand.

On the beaches of Guadalcanal, or wherever it was sandy, it was difficult to crank the generator. So the Navajos learned to hook the generator to the trunk of a coconut tree and then start cranking.

"One thing we learned at school," one Navajo once recalled, "was not to stay on the air any longer than was absolutely necessary. On Guadalcanal, that was a good lesson to have learned. The Japs would start shelling a spot as soon as you started operating."

Sometimes code talkers performed other tasks besides transmitting radio messages. During the invasion of Peleliu in the Palau Islands, the Marines suffered 2,000 casualties in the first two hours. Code talkers served as infantrymen, stretcher bearers, and B.A.R. men, lugging Browning Automatic Rifles. As one of the Navajos said, "In tough situations, you did what your commander asked you to do—with no questions asked!"

Many code talkers recall hair-raising experiences. A two-man team accompanied the earliest waves of Marines in the invasion of Tarawa. Their platoon commander kept ordering them forward. The men obeyed only to find they had gone too far ahead of the main unit and were pinned down in crossfire between American and Japanese lines.

One of the men spotted a foxhole and dived into it. He gasped when he saw the pit was occupied by a Japanese soldier. He fully expected to be shot or stabbed to death, but then he discovered the Japanese soldier was dead.

During the assault on the island of Iwo Jima, another pair of code talkers found themselves pinned down by enemy fire. They and the other Marines in the unit received orders to move forward. "At night," they were told, "when the first flare is fired, we're going to advance 200 yards."

When the flare went up, the two men started moving, crawling on their bellies and dragging their equipment. After about 15 minutes they stopped. They dug a foxhole using small shovels they carried. They were surprised it was so easy to dig.

The two men were kneeling in their foxhole when a second flare was fired. They were horror-stricken at what they saw. The flare cast eerie shadows from a row of tombstones just ahead of them. They had crawled into a graveyard. Worse, the foxhole they had dug was right over a grave. "Navajos aren't very happy in such a situation," one of the men was later to remark. "But we couldn't do anything about it."

One of the men hadn't slept for three days. His partner told him to try to get some sleep while he kept

NAVAJOS OPERATE A PORTABLE RADIO SET IN A CLEARING IN THE
DENSE JUNGLE OF BOUGAINVILLE IN THE SOLOMON ISLANDS IN THE
WESTERN PACIFIC. *(U.S. Marine Corps)*

watch. The man curled up at one end of the foxhole
and closed his eyes.

Then all of a sudden he started screaming. "Help!
Help!" he cried at the top of his lungs.

Because it was so dark, his partner couldn't see
what was happening. He grabbed a pistol in one
hand, a knife in the other. "What's wrong?" he
shouted. "What's wrong?"

Suddenly another flare arched into the sky, bathing the two men in light. A big sand crab lay across the neck of the man who had been trying to sleep. The crab's pincers were at the man's throat.

In the attack on Iwo Jima, the entire operation was directed by Navajo code. The Marine Corps command post was a battleship from which orders were transmitted to division commanders on the island.

During the first two days of the attack, six teams of Navajo radio operators worked around the clock and sent and received more than 800 messages.

"Were it not for the Navajos, the Marines would never have taken Iwo Jima," said Major Howard Connor, Signal Officer of the Third Marine Division.

When the war ended, most of the code talkers returned to their reservation homes. They received little praise and less acclaim. The men had agreed to keep themselves out of the spotlight, to seek no recognition for what they had done.

"If there was going to be another war," said Clare Thompson, one of the code talkers, "and this country needed our services, we all wanted to be ready and able to report back to duty. But if we were ever again to be as effective as we had been in the past, we had to keep the code a secret."

It was not until 1969 that anything was done to honor the code talkers. That year, when the Fourth Marine Division Association held its annual meeting in Chicago, each of the code talkers who attended was presented with a specially minted medallion in recognition of his contribution.

Since then the code talkers have formed their

own organization with headquarters in Window Rock, Arizona. At a reunion in 1971, President Richard Nixon hailed the code talkers, saying, "Their resourcefulness, tenacity, integrity, and courage saved the lives of countless men and women and sped the realization of peace for war-torn lands. Their achievements form a proud chapter in American military history."

7

BENDING
THE TRUTH

 World War II triggered sweeping changes in warfare. Motorized personnel carriers sped troops to the battlefront. Improvements in aircraft design led to aerial bombing and the use of paratroopers. Rockets and missiles came into use. And, at war's end, the atomic age dawned.

The use of propaganda as an important weapon was another change. All the major powers used propaganda, not only to influence the thinking and actions of their enemies, but also to stimulate desired behavior among their own citizens.

In Germany the Minister of Propaganda, Paul Joseph Goebbels, was elevated to a position second in rank only to Hitler himself. In Great Britain the head of the propaganda agency held cabinet rank. The United States established a propaganda agency called the Office of War Information, the OWI, for short. It was headed by Elmer Davis, a well-known journalist of the time.

The chief weapons used in the "war of words" were the leaflet, the loudspeaker, and the radio. A special military organization, the Psychological Warfare Division, was created to use these weapons.

The soldiers who staffed what came to be called the "psywar units" were unlike any soldiers ever known before. Instead of guns and ammunition, they were equipped with typewriters, portable printing presses, public address systems, and radio transmitters. They would arrange for massive leaflet airdrops over enemy positions. Or they would rig up loudspeakers, some with amplifying equipment that would carry sound for a mile or more, and call out messages to enemy soldiers in an effort to entice them to surrender.

On D-Day, Allied aircraft dropped more than 27 million leaflets on enemy positions along the invasion coast. A survey taken during the summer of 1944 disclosed that 90 percent of the German soldiers taken prisoner had propaganda leaflets in their possession.

Experts classify propaganda in three types—white, gray, or black. In white propaganda, no effort is made to conceal the source. An American propaganda leaflet urging German soldiers to surrender obviously originated from an American source. Tokyo Rose's broadcasts from Japan to American troops in the Pacific during the war is another example of white propaganda.

Gray propaganda revealed no source at all. When prepared by American psywar specialists, it usually took the form of newspapers or news-bearing leaflets

LOUDSPEAKER ON AMERICAN LIGHT TANK IN ZERBET, GERMANY, WAS USED TO TELL PEOPLE THE TOWN HAD FALLEN TO THE ALLIES, AND TO ORDER THE END OF RESISTANCE. *(National Archives)*

that were dropped over enemy positions. German soldiers had little doubt as to where the newspapers had originated, but they were so hungry for news they read them anyway.

Black propaganda was the most malicious. It pretended to originate from the enemy's own sources. One example was the small booklet prepared by Americans and distributed to German troops. It looked like an official German government medical handbook, giving information and advice on how to self-treat minor ailments and injuries. But the book's actual purpose was to instruct soldiers how to pretend to be ill and get themselves excused from active duty.

Radio was often used to spread black propaganda. Programs originating in England pretended to be

German stations broadcasting to the German people.

The man in charge of the Allies' black radio operation was Sefton Delmer, a British journalist. He had been born in Germany of British parents and, because he had lived in Germany as a young boy, he spoke German as well as he spoke English. During the 1930s Delmer lived in Berlin and worked as the Berlin correspondent for a London newspaper, *The Daily Express*. He knew many of the Nazi leaders personally.

To staff his station, Delmer scoured the German prison-of-war camps in England, seeking those prisoners who held anti-Nazi beliefs. He also obtained broadcasters and scriptwriters from among German men and women who had immigrated to England in the months just before the outbreak of war.

Delmer and his staff read German newspapers to keep abreast of what was happening in the principal German cities. They monitored conversations of German prisoners, not merely for information, but to pick up the latest slang. Delmer cautioned his staff to use the term "We Germans" in their broadcasts instead of "You Germans."

So that the broadcasts would be believable, Delmer had to make the programs sound even more patriotic than official German radio broadcasts. So he never failed to broadcast Hitler's speeches. He called for vigorous efforts on behalf of the German war effort. He constantly referred to American and British bombing planes as "terror raiders."

Once he had established credibility for his operation, Delmer began to slip in propaganda messages in a crafty manner. For example, an announcer

THIS PROPAGANDA LEAFLET WAS DISTRIBUTED TO GERMAN FAMILIES BY THE RUSSIANS DURING WORLD WAR II. THE CAPTION READS: "DAD IS DEAD! ACCUSE HITLER! IT'S HE WHO DID IT!" *(New York Public Library)*

would follow a report on the situation on the Russian front with the observation that, "It doesn't matter that 500 of our soldiers were killed in battle—or even 5,000. What is important is that we have a victory to present to our Fuehrer on his birthday." Such statements weakened the trust and confidence of German people in their leaders.

Sometimes Delmer created a rumor by denying it. In 1943, when German troops were being transported by air to North Africa to blunt an Allied thrust, Delmer beamed a black radio broadcast to German soldiers denying reports that transport planes were unsafe. "It is perfectly true," the broadcaster declared, "that there were some tragic incidents a while back when some planes crashed on taking off.

But the defect has been corrected." German soldiers boarding transport planes must surely have been shaking in their boots.

German sailors were also the target of black radio broadcasts. Early in the war German U-boats prowled the Atlantic, seeking to destroy allied shipping. German submarine crews at French ports were beamed broadcasts in which servicemen complained of glory-seeking U-boat commanders who were condemned for taking their submarines and crews on foolhardy missions mainly to earn promotions and awards for heroism. This placed doubts in the minds of the German submariners as to the leadership qualities of their commanding officers.

A LEAFLET BOMB FOR USE WITH A P-47 THUNDERBOLT. (National Archives)

Delmer's broadcasts often sought to undermine the authority of Nazi Party officials. He invented stories to demonstrate how they used their Party jobs for personal advantage. In one such broadcast, he told how the wives of Party officials (whom he named) in the town of Holstein learned from their husbands that the country's entire textile output was going to be needed for the war effort. The women immediately rushed to local department stores and bought up all available articles of clothing.

The broadcast caused the German commonfolk to question the conduct of their leaders. At the same time it implanted in their minds that a severe clothing shortage loomed.

Hitler realized that the radio broadcasts could seriously damage the morale of the German people. He ordered the broadcast channels to be jammed with static and interference, but the messages still got through. Hitler decreed that anyone who listened to the illegal stations would face imprisonment or death and he planted a rumor that a secret invention could detect those who listened to them.

At one stage German propagandists attempted to send black radio broadcasts to the United States. The programs featured two plain and simple midwesterners, Ed and Joe. They explained the poor quality of their broadcasts by telling audiences that their transmitting facilities were located in a trailer and that they had to move from place to place to elude the FBI. The broadcasts actually originated from the German port city of Bremen.

Ed and Joe often spoke out against President Franklin D. Roosevelt, condemning him as "that

PROPAGANDA LEAFLETS PRINTED BY THE ALLIES FOR DISTRIBUTION TO GERMAN TROOPS AND CIVILIAN POPULATION. *(National Archives)*

goof Roosevelt," but the broadcasts had little believability and listeners often laughed at what was meant to be serious.

Delmer was more successful, but sometimes his broadcasts did not have the effect he intended. In an effort to give his programs an authentic German flavor, he often played songs that had been recorded in German by Marlene Dietrich, a well-known American singer who had been born in Berlin. After the war Dietrich was accused of having sung for the German people over German radio stations. The charges angered her and she denied them heatedly.

People in Germany, however, insisted they heard her. They did not know, of course, that Dietrich's songs were part of Delmer's programming. And it was not until long after the war that Dietrich herself learned what was behind the accusations.

Other of Delmer's broadcasts came back to harm the Allied cause. One of his continuing goals was to paint local Nazi officials as corrupt or traitorous, and he would identify these officials by name and position.

After the war when some of these same officials were being tried as war criminals, they used Delmer's broadcasts as their defense. Delmer had declared that they were traitors, that they were helping to bring about the defeat of their nation. "That's right," said the accused war criminals, "that's exactly what we did." By claiming to have supported the Allied cause, they hoped to be declared innocent and escape punishment.

Delmer realized that in some instances there was no predicting the effects of his broadcasts. As he once observed, black radio could sometimes be a "black boomerang."

8

"GO FOR BROKE!"

ON A GRAY AND RAIN-SOAKED JULY afternoon in 1946, the 442nd Regimental Combat Team marched smartly down Constitution Avenue in Washington toward the White House and ceremonies honoring them on their return from war. They stood rigidly at attention while President Harry Truman fixed the Presidential Unit Citation to their regimental colors.

For the 442nd Combat Team, World War II was especially hard. They had been assigned to beat back the Germans in some of the toughest fighting of the European war.

That was only part of the story. The 442nd Combat Team were all Nisei—American-born Japanese—except for a sprinkling of officers. As Japanese-Americans, they also had to fight prejudice at home.

Executive Order 9066, signed by President Roosevelt, which went into effect 74 days after Pearl

Harbor, uprooted all Japanese-Americans on the Pacific Coast and assigned them to "internment camps" in isolated parts of Arkansas, Colorado, Utah, and other states for "the duration of the war." Each person was allowed to bring only the personal belongings that would fit into a suitcase or barracks bag.

Families were torn apart, personal relationships destroyed, and jobs lost. It has been estimated that the 110,000 Japanese-Americans affected by the order lost $400 million. No price tag can be put on the heartache they were made to endure.

In spite of Executive Order 9066, Nisei by the hundreds pleaded for the right to fight for their country. But the government refused to accept them. In fact, in March 1942, they were classified "4C, Enemy Aliens," by the Selective Service Board.

Six months after the Pearl Harbor attack, the War Department (it became the Department of Defense in 1949) agreed to put soldiers of Japanese roots in a special combat unit, the 100th Infantry Battalion. The excellent training record of the 100th Infantry Battalion convinced officials to form the 442nd Regimental Combat Team on February 1, 1943.

The Nisei were delighted. Tens of thousands of Japanese-Americans volunteered to join the unit. But the 442nd Combat Team could accommodate only 4,500 men.

On April 13, 1943, the first truckload of Nisei volunteers arrived at Camp Shelby, Mississippi, just outside Hattiesburg, to begin Army basic training. Most of the soldiers at Camp Shelby accepted the men of the 442nd Combat Team. But there were some who taunted them as "dirty Japs." They would sneer as they passed by. Others held the suspicion that the Nisei represented a "fifth column," that they were in sympathy with Japan and ready to act on the country's behalf at the first signal.

Yet the Nisei had never thought of themselves as being anything but American. In an effort to show their true feelings, they attacked basic training with startling fury.

"We set out to break every record in the Army," says Harry Takagi, now Washington representative of the Japanese Citizens League, but in 1943 a private with the 442nd Combat Team. "We felt we were fighting for the rights of all Japanese-Americans. If we failed, it would reflect discredit on all Japanese-Americans. We could not let that happen."

Nisei recruits struck out at each bayonet dummy as though it were an actual enemy. They scrambled over obstacle courses as if their lives depended on it. They would march in quick time until they seemed ready to drop—and then break into a brisk trot.

In combat exercises, Nisei recruits could never be convinced a hopeless position was a lost cause. They refused to give up. Any assault they launched usually ended in hand-to-hand combat.

Sometime during their training, the unit adopted an official motto—"Go for Broke!" It was an expression used by professional gamblers in Hawaii, and meant "Shoot the Works!"

Once training was completed, a few hundred of the Nisei were shipped to Africa to serve as replacements for soldiers in the 100th Infantry Battalion. But the bulk of the men waited and waited. Months went by. The Nisei griped about being stuck in the "Battle of Hattiesburg."

At last their turn came. In May 1944, the 442nd Combat Team sailed for Italy. At about the same time they arrived there, the first of a million-man invasion force was landing on the beaches of Normandy in France, about 600 miles to the northwest. The battle for western Europe was on.

The 442nd Combat Team was given an important but unglamorous role to play. They were to be part of the Allied force being used to keep German forces occupied in Italy. If the Germans were able to shift these units out of Italy and to the French front, it could jeopardize the prospects of victory in France.

Soldiers of the 442nd Combat Team went into action for the first time on June 26, 1944 at Suvereto, storming the town behind a wall of mortar fire. Nothing the Germans were able to do could stop them. The enemy finally broke and retreated.

During the next three months, the 442nd Combat Team pressed north, its Go for Broke attacks driving the enemy forces deeper into the mountains. One day became like every other. Towns and places all seemed the same—Sassetta, Castagneto, Orciano, Livorno.

Acts of bravery became common. Private First Class Kiichi Koda found enemy troops entrenched in a castle. After lobbing grenades through the castle windows, he led three of his buddies inside to finish the job with bullets and bayonets. Pfc. Koda died in the room-to-room fighting, but he and his buddies killed ten of the enemy. Three other Germans were captured and all of the enemy machine guns were

THREE MEMBERS OF THE 442ND REGIMENTAL COMBAT TEAM LOOK DOWN ON A FRENCH VALLEY NOT LONG BEFORE THE "LOST BATTAL-ION" BATTLE. (*U.S. Army*)

put out of action.

Staff Sergeant Kazuo Masuda was another Nisei hero. He crawled 200 yards through enemy fire to bring back a 60-mm mortar. But he was unable to retrieve the baseplate that supported the mortar when it was being fired. So Sergeant Masuda removed his helmet and used *it* as a baseplate. For 12 hours, repeatedly going back for more rounds, he kept the mortar firing. He single-handedly threw back two German counterattacks.

By mid-September 1944, the 442nd had wrested control from the Germans of every foot of the 50 rugged miles between Suvereto and Vecciano, north of Pisa. But what the men of the unit really wanted was a chance to participate in the bigger war in France.

The 442nd got that chance in October, when the unit received orders to join up with the 36th Division of the Seventh Army. The 36th Division had battered enemy strongholds throughout France on its drive to reach Germany. But now they were stalled in the bitter fighting in the Vosges Mountains of northeast France. Hitler's army, its back to the German border, had been ordered to "fight to the last man."

The terrain was more rugged than anything the men of the 442nd had experienced in Italy. The mountains rose many hundred feet from the valley floor and were covered with tall pines and thick underbrush. When the Germans lobbed an artillery shell toward them, it burst in the pines, showering the men with jagged shell fragments and deadly chunks of splintered wood.

The 442nd assaulted and took one hill after another. Sometimes they would lose as many as 20 men when a shell burst above the trees. And almost every time they gained a sizable piece of ground, the Germans would counterattack.

Day and night, the enemy guns never stopped firing. Winter was approaching and many of the men spent their nights in foxholes half-filled with frozen water.

The 442nd had not been in France for very long when it received one of the toughest assignments of the war. The 1st Battalion of the 141st Infantry Regiment (36th Division) had gotten cut off and now was surrounded by German troops near a hill in the Vosges Mountains. The battalion had been ordered to fight its way back, but had been unable to do so.

Communications and supply lines to the unit had been cut. The Germans were closing in on all sides. The 279-man unit had become known as the "lost battalion." The 442nd Combat Team was given the mission of rescuing them. The men moved out in the hours before daybreak. When the Germans became aware of the 442nd's advance, they began pounding them with everything they had—artillery, mortars, machine guns, and hand grenades. But the 442nd pressed the attack, trying to cut a path through the enemy lines.

Staff Sergeant Gordon Yamashiro crept up on a road block and attacked a nearby machine gun nest with his rifle. He killed the three men manning the machine gun. A second machine gun opened fire on him. He attacked it and killed the second crew.

Sergeant Yamashiro began laying down a screen of fire to cover the advance of his men. Then a sniper killed him. But he had driven a wedge in the enemy's defense. His men charged, killing every enemy soldier who didn't surrender, and they took the roadblock.

Meanwhile, the situation was growing worse for the "lost battalion." Artillery had fired in chocolate bars and emergency rations to the trapped men, but they were becoming desperately low on water and medical supplies. Ammunition was running out. The battalion could not hold out much longer.

The 442nd was ordered to "push through at any cost." As the men picked their way along narrow paths and ridges, they hit a minefield. They decided to go through it. "Go for broke!" some of the men shouted. Before they got beyond the minefield, German guns opened up on them. But they did not fall back.

Men fired from the hip as they advanced. They rushed in with hand grenades. They fixed bayonets and charged German positions.

By the end of the fourth day, the 442nd was less than half a mile from the "lost battalion." They had destroyed most of the enemy forces on the mountain. But half of their men were dead or wounded.

On the afternoon of the next day, following a heavy artillery barrage that had been launched in their support, the first men of the 442nd reached the "lost battalion." "There were a lot of tears but not much cheering," one survivor recalled. "We were all too tired to cheer."

For the next several months, the 442nd rested. New men were assigned to the unit to replace those who had been killed or wounded.

In March 1945, the 442nd received orders to return to Italy. German troops were holding the Gothic Line, a chain of interlocking defensive positions across the barren mountains of northern Italy. The 442nd was assigned to drive the enemy from the westernmost peaks.

For sheer heroism, their first strike, an assault on fortifications atop Mount Folgorita, may be unmatched in military history. Two units of the 442nd began a wide flanking attack, climbing almost straight up, mostly on their hands and knees. Wearing full combat gear, they scaled the mountains in total darkness. Complete silence had to be maintained. Medals and dogtags were wrapped with tape. Coins had to be tossed away. No one could speak.

Some men slipped and fell to their death. But no one cried out and no one turned back.

At the summit, they took the startled German troops by surprise. Their final charge killed or scattered the enemy defenders.

On one ridge, Private First Class Sadao Munemori's squad was pinned down by machine gun fire. Private Munemori successfully attacked two of the machine guns. As he was returning to his men, a German hand grenade struck his helmet, bounced off, and rolled toward two of his men. Private Munemori dived on the grenade, smothering the blast with his body. He gave up his life rather than see his men die.

PRESIDENT HARRY S. TRUMAN AWARDS THE PRESIDENTIAL UNIT CITATION TO THE 442ND REGIMENTAL COMBAT TEAM. *(U.S. Army)*

By the early part of May, the 442nd Combat Team received the Presidential Distinguished Unit Citation from President Truman, marking the seventh time the unit had won the award. In 20 months of combat, the 442nd Combat Team had earned over 18,000 individual awards, including one Medal of Honor (awarded to Private First Class Munemori), more than 9,400 Purple Hearts, 52 Distinguished Service Crosses, and 588 Silver Stars. The Niseis' record was unexcelled.

9

THE BIG LIE

On JUNE 6, 1944, the biggest invasion in history was launched across the English Channel into France. Almost 3,000,000 American, British, and Canadian troops took part. They were supported by a fleet of more than 5,000 ships and 11,000 aircraft.

Minesweepers went first, clearing the coastal waters of explosive charges. Battleships, cruisers, and destroyers blasted enemy fortifications with their gunfire. Bombers attacked from the sky.

Paratroopers cut railroad lines, blew up bridges, and seized landing fields. Gliders brought in jeeps, small tanks, and light artillery.

At 6:30 A.M., under gray skies, the first waves of infantry waded ashore at carefully-planned points along 50 miles of French coastline in the province of Normandy. Americans landed at beaches with the code names Utah and Omaha. At Utah, only pockets of resistance were encountered, but at Omaha the

A PORTION OF THE D-DAY INVASION FORCE. *(U.S. Navy)*

Germans fought fiercely.

Gold, Juno, and Sword were the code names of beaches where the British landed. At Juno, they were supported by Canadian units. British and Canadians were successful on all three beaches, although at points the Germans fought with the savagery the Americans faced at Omaha.

In the days that followed, the Allies poured hundreds of thousands more men into the ever-widening beachheads. Tons of supplies and tens of thousands of vehicles were landed along with the troops.

A long struggle remained. France and other German holdings throughout Europe, and Germany itself, still had to be fought for and won. But the Allies had gained a vital foothold from which the final assault on Hitler's "Fortress Europe" could be launched.

There were many reasons how and why the invasion had succeeded against a tough and experienced enemy. One fact, however, stands out: the Normandy invasion came as a surprise to the German defenders.

Field Marshal Carl Gerd von Rundstedt, who commanded the German forces in Western Europe, held back from committing all of his ground troops and firepower. This was not the real invasion, he thought. Von Rundstedt was waiting for a second Allied thrust, an assault that never occurred.

Von Rundstedt believed that the "real" invasion was to take place at Calais, about 100 miles to the northeast, which was exactly what the Allies wanted von Rundstedt to believe! In the months that preceded the invasion, Allied intelligence agents had gone to enormous lengths to establish in the minds of the German High Command that the assault on Normandy was merely a feint, a soft jab before the knockout punch. And they succeeded.

The Allies began to plan an assault across the English Channel as early as 1942. Deciding exactly where to land was the first order of business.

Calais was the obvious choice. The distance across the English Channel at Calais was only about 20 miles, while the Normandy beaches were more than 75 miles from England. But the terrain inland from Calais was a problem. The many rivers and streams that crisscrossed the area would have slowed the progress of the attacking force.

Brittany, the large peninsula at France's northwest corner, was also considered as the invasion target. But it was too far from England.

Normandy had several advantages. It was in easy range of fighter planes and aircraft needed for ground support. It offered plenty of space for tactical

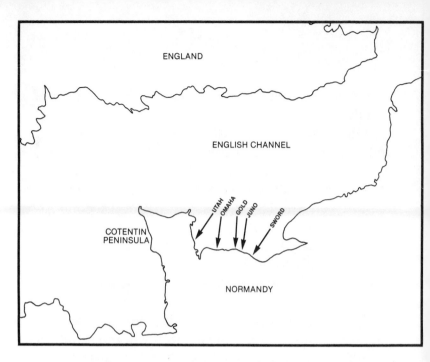

ALLIED LANDING ZONES ON D-DAY. *(Neil Katine, Herb Field Art Studio)*

maneuvering. And the area selected for the landings was flanked by the Seine and Orne Rivers, which would offer some measure of natural protection.

Once the Allies decided upon Normandy, the next task was to keep it a secret. If the Germans knew in advance where the Allies were going to land, they would mass troops and guns against the invasion force, making it easy to push the troops back into the sea.

At first the Allies considered launching an attack on Calais at the same time as the Normandy assault. The Calais attacking force would be much smaller and only for the purpose of drawing the Germans' attention from what was happening at Normandy. But this plan would never fool the Germans. They would realize from the small number of troops and landing craft that it was not the real invasion force.

Then the Allies developed the "Big Lie" to feed the Germans:

> *The main Allied assault would be launched against Calais, and it would come six weeks after the landings at Normandy. The Normandy attack was to be a decoy to divert the Germans from the main attack that was to follow.*

The Allies figured if they could get the Germans to believe this lie it would go a long way toward making D-Day a success. The Germans would hold back some of their forces from Normandy, waiting for the attack on Calais.

To entice the Germans into believing the lie, the Allies pretended to be making invasion preparations much farther to the east, opposite Calais. The build up for the real attack was to be kept secret.

The Allies wanted the Germans to think the U.S. First Army would be landing at Calais. Troops of the First Army were transferred to the coastal region of England just opposite Calais.

A commanding officer had to be assigned to the First Army Group, one who would seem believable in that post to the Germans. The name of General Omar Bradley was suggested, but Bradley was scheduled to land in Normandy with the real assault forces. If the Germans saw Bradley in France, they would realize something was wrong.

Then it was decided to choose General George Patton to lead the First Army Group. Patton was already in charge of the Third Army, but the Third Army was not scheduled to land in France until more than a month after D-Day. By that time there would be no need for the deception.

To transport the First Army and its equipment to Calais, a fleet of fake landing craft was created to be displayed along the rivers of southeast England. It included countless dummy landing craft for tanks, known as "Bigbobs," and dummy landing craft for the troops, called "Wetbobs."

The Bigbobs, 160 feet long and 30 feet wide, were made of painted canvas strips lashed to steel tubing. They were equipped with wheels so they could be pushed from the assembly sheds to the water. Once in the water they were supported by floats.

The Wetbobs were smaller and made of inflatable rubber. Twenty Wetbobs, rolled up like carpets, could be carried in a single truck.

After more than 250 Bigbobs and Wetbobs had been placed in position, camouflage experts were taken aloft to look them over. They decided the dummy craft didn't look real enough. To make them appear more genuine, clotheslines were strung on some of them with washing hung out to dry.

When a reconnaissance plane approached and was picked up on radar, coastal antiaircraft batteries were automatically put on alert and Allied fighter squadrons were sent into the air. But once the Bigbobs and Wetbobs were in place, these plans were revised. Fighter planes were kept on the ground so as not to scare a reconnaissance plane away. And although the antiaircraft fired at the plane, the gunners were told to shoot too low.

When a German reconnaissance plane returned home, its cameras contained hundreds of photo-

U. S. TROOPS ABOARD A LANDING CRAFT BEFORE INVASION OF FRANCE.
(*U.S. Navy*)

graphs of landing craft in Dover Harbor. German intelligence experts examining the pictures would draw the conclusion that the craft must be intended for landings at Calais. Certainly they couldn't be intended for Normandy; it was too far away for such boats.

To add to the deception, various units of the First Army broadcast fake messages to each other. The Allies knew that the Germans monitored such radio traffic.

Often the fake messages would comment on local weather conditions. This made them sound more authentic. And when fog blanketed the English Channel between Calais and the southeast coast, broadcasts were cancelled, giving the Germans the impression that training exercises had been called off because of bad weather.

At one time in the weeks before D-Day, 20 units of the First Army were transmitting fake radio messages. Since most of this radio traffic originated only a short distance from the enemy forces, less than 50 miles in most cases, it was very easy to monitor.

In the early years of the war, the Allied forces had worked diligently on the development of fake tanks, vehicles, and guns to deceive the Germans. All this knowledge and experience was to be put to use in promoting the D-Day hoax. Take the case of the Sherman tank, one of the most formidable of Allied weapons. Dummy Sherman tanks were available in three different versions—folding, inflatable, and mobile.

The folding model was made of plywood sections that were painted in standard tank colors and bore tank markings. The parts for several folding models could be carried in one truck and assembled on the site.

The inflatable models were made of lengths of rubber tubing. When filled with air, the tubing became a rigid tank skeleton. By fastening on strips of

(TOP) BODY ASSEMBLY FOR A DUMMY TANK IS LAID OUT BEFORE IN-FLATING. (National Archives) (MIDDLE) BRITISH SOLDIERS INFLATE THE TURRET OF A DUMMY TANK. INFLATED BODY ASSEMBLY IS IN BACK-GROUND. (National Archives) (BOTTOM) INFLATED DUMMY TANK IS PLACED IN POSITION UNDER CAMOUFLAGE NETTING. (National Archives)

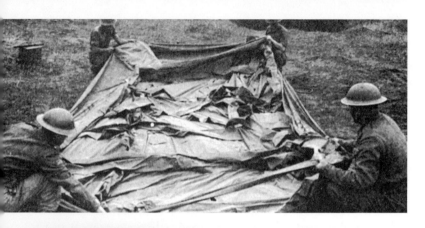

canvas, the result was an object with a tank shape. It did not look very much like a real tank up close, of course, but from the air it was difficult to tell an inflatable from the genuine article. Not only were tanks created in this fashion, but also big trucks, armored vehicles, guns, and even aircraft.

The mobile Sherman tank consisted of a tank-shaped framework of light steel tubing covered with canvas. The various features of a tank—the caterpillar treads, the turret, etc.—were painted on the canvas. Fitted over the body of a jeep, it gave the appearance of a tank moving into position quickly.

The deception had several defects, however. The fake tanks could not cross ditches or climb steep banks. They did not send up thick clouds of dust when crossing open terrain. And they did not make the loud rumbling sounds real tanks made. But these flaws didn't matter. From distances of 350 yards and more, the mobile Sherman tank dummies looked authentic.

In the spring of 1944, when German reconnaissance planes made daily flights over southeast England, their cameras recorded what appeared to be enormous buildups of troops and equipment. There were tent cities where troops of the First Army were quartered. Tanks, vehicles, and guns were lined row upon row in vast staging areas.

Meanwhile, farther to the west, where the real invasion force was being assembled, strict security precautions were observed. A ten-mile strip of coastline became a restricted zone. No one was allowed to enter or leave the area without permission from top authority.

All new buildings in the area used for housing or training the invasion force were camouflaged by painted patterns of foliage to hide them from German reconnaissance planes. Tents were kept darkened at night. Only smokeless stoves could be used in cookhouses. All troops were issued khaki-colored towels and underclothing. White cloth could too easily be spotted from the sky.

The Big Lie also directly involved General Montgomery, who had previously headed the British Eighth Army in North Africa and now commanded the British forces who were being massed for the D-Day assault.

Clifton James, an actor, was called upon to impersonate Montgomery. James looked a great deal like the general except for a missing middle finger on his right hand. That was camouflaged by having him wear gloves.

James was assigned to Montgomery's staff to study the general at close range. At night in his room he practiced the way Montgomery walked and carried himself. He took to clasping his hands behind his back during a discussion the way Montgomery did. He frequently carried a Bible, another trait for which Montgomery was well known.

James had long conversations with Montgomery so he could become familiar with the quality and cadence of his voice. The general had a habit of selecting his words with great care. James developed that habit.

When James felt he was ready, he was given a test. A group of senior intelligence officers assembled and James was brought in to address them. The officers marveled at how closely the actor resembled Monty and how well he duplicated the general's crisp man-to-man style of speaking.

Toward the end of May, with D-Day about a week away, James was given a crucial assignment. He was flown to Gibraltar, the British fortress and seaport near the southern tip of Spain that guards the entrance to the Mediterranean Sea. There he was met at the plane and driven to Government House in an open car. The Allies wanted to be sure that the many German agents in Gibraltar learned of the famous general's arrival. Sir Ralph Eastwood, the governor and a close friend of Montgomery's, was in on the secret.

During his stay in Gibraltar, Montgomery's impersonator spoke often of a mysterious "Plan 300," which he described as an assault on the Mediterranean coast of France that would be mounted across the Mediterranean from the northern coast of Africa. Eastwood arranged for certain Spanish businessmen, known to be in contact with German agents, to overhear James discussing Plan 300. When James left Gibraltar his destination was Algiers, capital of Algeria on Africa's north coast.

The Allies did not care whether the Germans believed that Plan 300 might or might not be real. (It was not.) Their main objective was to establish General Montgomery's physical presence in Gibraltar. If the Germans believed that he was there and that he was embarking on a tour of North Africa, they were likely to conclude that an invasion across the English Channel into France was not planned for the immediate future, for such an undertaking could never be scheduled without Monty's full participation.

By the middle of May there were indications that the Germans were beginning to believe the "Big Lie." In his report for the week ending May 21, just 16 days before the invasion was to take place, Field Marshal von Rundstedt named southeast England—the area opposite Calais—as one point from which the invasion might be launched.

Allied bombing planes pounded the French coast in the weeks before the invasion. The bombs they dropped were real, of course, but the bombing pattern was meant to mislead the enemy. For every bomb dropped on Normandy, two were dropped on Calais.

Day in and day out this rule was followed religiously. Somewhere, the Allies knew, a German intelligence officer was keeping count of the bombs showering down, attempting to establish a pattern to the attacks. His calculations would show that Calais was deemed by Allied bombing planes to be twice as important as Normandy. The Allies hoped the Germans would draw the obvious conclusion.

About a week before the invasion the troops began leaving the sprawling camps where they were quartered. They were brought by trucks to huge assembly areas near the ports from which they were to embark. The assembly areas were called "sausages" because they had an oblong shape with rounded ends.

When the men entered the sausages, they still did not know where they were going to land. They were given photos of the beaches, which had been taken at sea level, and showed the coast exactly as the men would see it as their landing craft approached. But there was no indication of where each particular piece of coast was located.

The men were also given maps, but these did not contain any clues as to their destination. The rivers of Normandy had been given Russian names. The city of Caen, about ten miles inland from the coast, was labeled Warsaw.

A few days before the invasion all the planning and secrecy were suddenly placed in jeopardy. A stiff breeze blew through an open window of the British War Office in London and whisked away 12 copies of Top Secret instructions involving the invasion. The sheets of paper drifted down into a crowd of pedestrians on the sidewalk below.

Office workers raced down to the street in a frantic effort to recover the papers. Eleven of the missing sheets were retrieved right away. The twelfth could not be found.

The street was scoured again, then a third time. The missing document remained lost. Officers went through torment believing the worst, that the information would somehow find its way into German hands, wrecking the invasion. Two agonizing hours passed. Then a British sentry, standing duty on the opposite side of the street, turned in the missing sheet of paper. A stranger had handed it to him, he said. No one ever learned the identity of the individual who held the fate of the invasion in his hands.

On D-Day itself, more deceptive tactics were used. Dummy parachutists were dropped to draw German troops from fortified positions or from areas where real parachutists were set to attack.

AN AMERICAN SOLDIER PUTS THE FINISHING TOUCHES TO A DUMMY AIRPLANE. *(National Archives)*

Each dummy was a full-sized representation of a human figure, clothed in an Army uniform. The dummy's parachute was the real thing.

There were four drops of dummy parachutists on D-Day. One of the biggest of the drops, code named Titanic I, involved 200 dummies. They were dropped near the town of Yvetot about five hours before the first Allied troops were due to hit the nearby beaches. They were meant to draw German defenders away from their beach positions.

To get the Germans to believe that the drop was the real thing, Allied military experts fitted the dummies with timing devices that triggered recordings of battle noises, sounds of machine gun fire, and exploding grenades. The sounds were so real that anyone in the area would quickly seek cover.

Another part of the deception involved dropping a group of intelligence agents into the area just before the dummy 'chutists were released. The agents put life into the attack, firing on German troops or vehicles that entered the area. But they were instructed to allow some enemy soldiers to escape to spread news of the paratroop landing.

Once the invasion began, von Rundstedt reacted just as the Allies had hoped. While German opposition was strong at some points, by nightfall of the first day Allied forces held several beachheads along the Normandy shore. In the days that followed, no serious counterattack developed.

Wilhelm Keitel, Hitler's chief of staff, replying to reporters the day after he was sentenced to death as a war criminal at Nuremberg, said this about D-Day: "German military intelligence knew nothing of the real state of Allied preparations. Even when craft carrying Allied troops were approaching the coast of Normandy, the highest state of alert was not ordered."

As late as June 25, almost three weeks after the first landings, von Rundstedt continued to believe the main Allied assault was targeted on Calais, and he continued to hold back many thousands of troops.

Had they been sent into action, would these German troops have tipped the scales in the first critical hours of D-Day? One can only guess. But one fact is certain. The Big Lie and the Germans' acceptance of it made the Allied task of gaining a foothold in the Normandy beaches much less difficult and contributed to saving many thousands of lives. For that reason alone, it ranks as one of the war's important triumphs.

10

V FOR
VENGEANCE

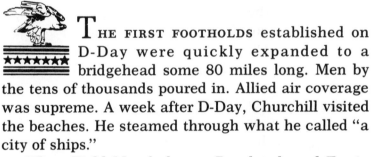 THE FIRST FOOTHOLDS established on D-Day were quickly expanded to a bridgehead some 80 miles long. Men by the tens of thousands poured in. Allied air coverage was supreme. A week after D-Day, Churchill visited the beaches. He steamed through what he called "a city of ships."

When Field Marshals von Rundstedt and Erwin Rommel, commanders of the German forces, realized they had failed to prevent the landing, they planned to withdraw their forces and establish a defensive line farther to the east, a move that would shorten their supply lines.

Hitler, however, would not permit any withdrawal. Von Rundstedt and Rommel met with him at Soissons, about halfway between Paris and the Belgian border, 11 days after the Allied landings. "You must stay where you are," Hitler told his generals.

They, in turn, warned him that it was disastrous

to hold a line so far to the west. Hitler dismissed the warning and told them of a secret weapon he was about to unveil—the flying bomb. The Fuehrer believed it would change the course of the war.

The generals urged Hitler to use the new weapon against the invasion beaches or the ports along the British coast that were supplying the Allied forces. Hitler had a different strategy. He planned to bombard London instead, believing this strategy would "convert the English to peace."

The flying bomb that Hitler talked of was a small, pilotless craft that flew a preset course. Each carried a one-ton package of explosives.

The miniature craft flew at an altitude of about 2,000 feet, traveling 350 miles an hour. Its maximum range was about 150 miles. When its fuel supply gave out, it dived for ground, exploding on impact.

These weapons rained death and destruction upon London for the next two and a half months. They arrived at random intervals, so Londoners never felt safe. The Germans called the weapon *Vergeltungswaffe Eins* (Vengeance Weapon One). To the Americans and British, they were known as V-1s.

The V-1 was powered by a special jet engine, a pulse jet, which made a low, stuttering sound. Because of its distinctive sound, the British nicknamed the weapon the "buzz bomb."

The reign of terror did not reduce London to ruins nor did it come close to defeating the British, but it killed many people and frightened millions more.

To thwart the V-1, the British installed antiaircraft guns along the coast so the small planes could

10-1

BRITISH FIGHTER
PLANE (RIGHT) TRAILS
A V-2 ROCKET ACROSS
SOUTHERN ENGLAND.
(*United Press International*)

be fired upon as they approached. Fighter planes were dispatched to shoot them down over the English Channel. A ring of big helium-filled balloons, each resembling a blimp, went up around London. But still the V-1s got through.

Advancing Allied armies eventually captured the V-1 launching sites in France, ending the attacks. More than 40,000 people, mostly civilians, were killed or injured by the V-1s.

A GIRL VICTIM OF A ROCKET BOMB IN LONDON. (*United Press International*)

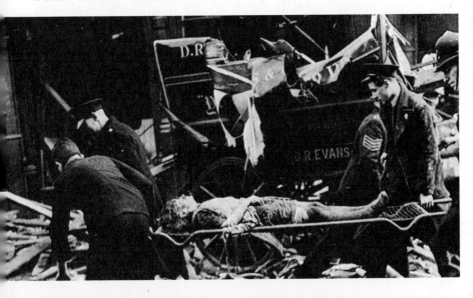

A V-2 THAT CRASHED AFTER TAKEOFF IS EXAMINED BY A CANADIAN SOLDIER (RIGHT) AND A MEMBER OF THE FRENCH RESISTANCE MOVEMENT. *(United Press International)*

The terror was not over, however. From bases in the Netherlands, the Germans began firing an advanced version of the V-1, called the V-2. The first of these was launched in September of 1944.

The V-2 was much faster than the V-1, capable of a speed of 3,300 miles per hour, meaning that it traveled faster than the speed of sound and arrived without the slightest warning. No one was aware of its presence until there was a deafening explosion and an entire building or city square was blasted out of existence. The V-2 ranks as one of the most frightening weapons of war ever devised.

The Germans mounted V-2 launching platforms on railroad flatcars and moved them from place to place. Not until the Allied troops captured the sites where the V-2s were being manufactured did the attacks end. That was in March, 1945. In all, more than 12,000 V-2s hit England, causing almost 10,000 casualties.

The V-1s and V-2s never accomplished what Hitler expected, nor did they change the course of the war. Nevertheless, when the last of the vengeance weapons had fallen, Allied military experts breathed a sigh of relief. What would have happened, they wondered, had the use of V-1s and V-2s begun earlier, even three or four weeks earlier? They surely would have crippled Allied plans for the invasion and they could have extended the war for months, perhaps even a year or more.

Hitler had begun developing these weapons late in the 1930s, not long after he gained control of the Nazi party. They would have been available for his use much earlier had it not been for a strange twist of fate.

The story of the V-1s and V-2s begins after World War I with the Treaty of Versailles. The treaty barred the Germans from producing guns or artillery, but the treaty said nothing about the development and production of rockets for military use.

The Germans decided to take advantage of this loophole. A civilian engineer, Wernher von Braun, who had experimented with rockets as a child, was named to head Germany's rocket production project.

In 1937, the Society for Space Travel, a group headed by von Braun, founded a research center at Peenemünde, a small island in the Baltic Sea just off Germany's northern coast. Peenemünde was farming and dairy country, a quiet and peaceful region of thatch-roofed homes and green meadows.

Von Braun's first successful experiments involved the use of rockets in connection with aircraft takeoffs. These eventually led to the development of jet-powered aircraft.

With that work behind him, von Braun began the development of a long range, pilotless rocket that would be able to carry a two-ton warhead. Launched in a high arc to a height of more than 20 miles, it would travel to its target at twice the speed of sound, its liquid fuel propellant carrying it a distance of about 200 miles. It could be neither seen nor heard until its warhead struck the ground, exploding like an aerial bomb.

In March 1939, just a few months before he was to order the invasion of Poland, Hitler witnessed a test of the rocket. He was not impressed. It was so unpredictable in flight that the engineers who launched it were not sure where it was going to come down.

The work at Peenemünde continued in utmost secrecy, however, with more than 1200 engineers assigned to the project. By late 1942, V-2 rockets were being test fired on a regular basis, but because the weapon sometimes flew erratically, more work was needed.

The Allies were aware that something was afoot at Peenemünde. Danish fishermen told of an unusual amount of activity on the island. Reconnaissance planes were assigned to take photographs of the area.

In May 1943, one such plane took a baffling photo at Peenemünde. It showed a tiny blurred speck in the shape of a miniature airplane parked on an inclined ramp. In the vicinity of the ramp, the ground was blackened as if by a hot blast.

At about the same time that British intelligence agents were puzzling over the photograph, Stanley

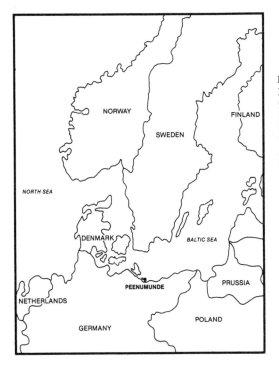

Lovell, an American intelligence officer, came upon some equally bewildering information concerning Peenemünde. Based in Washington, Lovell was the Director of Research and Development of the Office of Strategic Services, the OSS, the highly secret sabotage and intelligence arm of the U.S. government.

Lovell was reading copies of messages that had been received from OSS agents around the world, when one caught his eye. It was from an agent in Switzerland and it reported a conversation the agent had had with a worker who had escaped from German-occupied France to Switzerland.

The report ended with these words: "Workman told following improbable story: Said he was forced to guard casks of water from Rjukan in Norway to island of Peenemünde in Baltic Sea."

Why would a French lab worker have been guarding water? Lovell asked himself. Then he recalled a scientific discussion he had attended the week before. During the discussion, the term "heavy water" had been used. It had been described as an element necessary to the production of a nuclear or atomic bomb. Heavy water would, indeed, be water worth guarding.

Lovell then learned that Rjukan was the site of one of the biggest hydroelectric plants in all of Europe. As such, it was one of a handful of plants capable of producing heavy water. If the Germans were sending heavy water to Peenemünde, Lovell concluded, then Peenemünde must be where Germany was developing its atomic bomb.

Lovell recalled Hitler saying, "We will have a weapon to which there is no answer." An atomic bomb, Lovell knew, could be such a weapon. When Lovell reported his theory to his superiors, they were skeptical. But leading atomic scientists of the day believed him.

Lovell was flown to London to meet OSS officials there. They were impressed with what he had to say. If the Germans were developing an atomic bomb at Peenemünde, they had to be stopped immediately.

On the night of August 17, 1943, a huge fleet of four-engined Lancaster bombers took to the air. The next day, the British Air Ministry issued this official communiqué:

> Last night aircraft of the Bomber Command made a heavy attack in bright moonlight on the research and development establishment at

Peenemünde, 60 miles northeast of Stettin. The establishment is the largest and most important of its kind in Germany. A great number of aircraft were encountered along the route. Several were destroyed.

Later it was learned that enemy fighters had battered the raiders along a great part of the route, and 41 of 300 bombing planes had been lost. But those that managed to reach the target ripped the research center apart.

Daily newspapers in the United States spoke of the destruction that had been wrought at "Germany's mystery plant." More than a thousand people were killed in the raid and all above-ground installations were leveled.

While the bombing planes derailed the V-1 and V-2 programs, they did not put an end to them. Production of the weapons continued underground.

It was not until after the war that the mystery of the heavy water being shipped to Peenemünde was unraveled. Lovell learned from the chief of the hydroelectric plant at Rjukan that, for reasons of security, guards were told that heavy water shipments from the plant were headed for Peenemünde. While the ships carrying the heavy water came close to Peenemünde, they never actually landed there but continued to the German port of Wolgast. From Wolgast, the heavy water was sent by rail to plants where nuclear research was going on.

Thus, by trying to deceive the Allies, the Germans made the mistake of focusing attention on Peenemünde. The bombing raid that followed has

(LEFT) DR. WERNHER VON BRAUN, ONE-TIME HEAD OF GERMANY'S ROCKET DEVELOPMENT PROGRAM, PICTURED IN THE UNITED STATES IN 1977. *(National Aeronautics & Space Administration)* (RIGHT) TESTING A V-2 ROCKET AT CAPE CANAVERAL, FLORIDA, IN 1950. *(National Aeronautics and Space Administration)*

been ranked as one of the most important of the war.

There is one other strange twist to this story. After the Allied forces captured Peenemünde and the war in Europe had ended, Wernher von Braun and more than 125 other German scientists who had worked on the V-1 and V-2 programs joined forces with American scientists who were working on the U.S. rocket program. Thus, the development of Hitler's terrible vengeance weapons eventually led to man's first landing on the moon and many of the other space achievements that followed.

11

DOUBLE CROSS

 Double agents are as common to war-time spying as codes and cameras. A golden era in the practice of having one spy serve two countries occurred during World War II, with the British becoming masters of the art.

The double agent section of the British Secret Intelligence Service was known as M15. This department has been made famous by the popular hero of novels and motion pictures, James Bond.

Double agents aided the British in many ways. They were able to obtain information about German secret codes and military plans. If, for example, agents were asked to gather detailed information about the antiaircraft defenses in southeast England, it could mean that that area was about to come under attack.

Sometimes the British were able to influence German military planning through their double agents. During 1943, for instance, German officials began to query several of their agents about what preparations had been made in England for gas warfare. The British instructed the agents to send back glowing accounts of what had been done, giving the impression that gas warfare would be of greater advantage to the British than the Germans. The subject of gas warfare was dropped by the Germans, never to be brought up again.

"By means of the double agent system," a noted British historian wrote after the war, "we actively ran and controlled the German espionage system in this country [England]." That statement is incredible—but true.

The most successful of the British double agents was known by the code name Garbo. He was a Spaniard whose brother happened to be in Paris when the Germans marched in. His brother was taken into custody by the Gestapo, the German secret police, and never heard from again. Garbo became a dedicated anti-Nazi as a result.

In January 1941, Garbo offered his services as a spy to officials at the British embassy in Madrid. The British turned him down.

His next move was to offer himself to the Germans. He reasoned that if he could become a member of the German spy network, he would be of greater value to the British and they would undoubtedly reconsider the idea of hiring him.

Garbo sought out the Germans, telling them he could get himself sent to England by the Spanish. The Germans hired him, provided him with money, secret ink, a radio transmitter, and the addresses of residences that he could use while in England.

But Garbo never bothered to go to England. He settled down in Lisbon, Portugal, and from there began filing false reports to Germany about the British. He based his messages on information he got from English newspapers, old guidebooks, and out-of-date railway timetables.

Garbo would report imaginary military traffic moving along the various railway lines, describing newly erected barbed wire and fortifications he had sighted along the way.

If the Germans asked him to find out if certain British army units were being transported from one place to another, Garbo would never fail to report having seen them. He would make his response sound even more believable by reporting he had sighted the troops a second time several days later.

Garbo's guesses and deductions were often amazingly accurate. More and more the Germans came to depend on him. He even created two imaginary sub-agents who reported to him from different parts of England.

Garbo was able to be successful even though he was not comfortable in the use of the English language. He knew only a few English names, and the country's monetary system, involving pence, shillings, and pounds, was a mystery to him. Preparing expense accounts for himself and the agents he employed was never easy.

Early in 1942, Garbo reported to the Germans about the preparations the English were making in Liverpool to send an enormous convoy to Malta, the tiny British island colony in the Mediterranean between Sicily and the North African coast. The Germans began at once to make plans to intercept it.

The British observed that the Germans were transferring large numbers of ships and planes to the central Mediterranean. They couldn't understand why. Then they learned of Garbo's messages. The British decided it was time to hire Garbo, and he was smuggled over to England, where the Germans thought he had been for the previous nine months.

Garbo continued sending messages to Germany, all of them as fictional as *The Wizard of Oz*. Yet the Germans never doubted the reports. British intelligence agents started making plans to develop an entire network of imaginary agents, with Garbo acting as its chief.

The British called the subagents "notional" agents. They existed only as a notion, an idea; they existed only in the mind.

The notional agent in Liverpool, the one who had spotted the Malta convoy, posed a problem for Garbo and his British employers. The Allies were making massive preparations in Liverpool for Operation Torch, the invasion of North Africa. Garbo's agent there, because of the job he held, would be able to observe the Allied buildup. If he failed to report what was going on, the Germans might begin to question Garbo and the entire network.

Garbo solved the problem by telling the Germans that the agent had become seriously ill. Reports from the man stopped. Garbo hurried to Liverpool to find out what was wrong. There he learned the poor man had died. A death notice was placed in the *Liverpool Daily Post*, and when it appeared Garbo clipped it out and sent it to his German contacts.

Other notional agents were created to replace the agent who had died. Garbo and his British co-workers lived the lives of the imaginary agents, creating personality characteristics for each of them. Some reported on the basis of rumors, beginning their messages with, "I've heard that," or, "I believe." Others stuck strictly to the facts.

Some agents would get ill. Some would disclose family problems they were having. Some would complain about the money they were receiving—the Germans paid all of the agents—and ask for more. Some would get arrested by the British authorities. Some would quit, saying they were afraid of getting arrested. But all were entirely fictional.

The Germans continued to trust Garbo. They provided him with the latest secret codes and the most sophisticated radio equipment available.

By the spring of 1944, Garbo headed a network of 14 notional agents. They were stationed in such towns as Glasgow, Dover, Brighton, Exeter, and Swansea.

Garbo and his spy network made an important contribution to the success of D-Day. For months prior to the landings, he reported that Allied troops were being assembled in huge numbers in the southeast of England and in Scotland. This gave the Germans a false impression of where the landings were actually to occur. About three weeks before the invasion began, the Allies captured a book of secret instructions that had been issued to all German commanders in the field. The maps it contained showed Allied troop concentrations exactly as they had been reported by Garbo.

Even after the landings had begun, Garbo continued to report massed Allied troops in southeastern England. This helped to convince the Germans that they should keep a good part of their forces in reserve, and wait for additional landings, which, of course, never took place.

In December 1944, Garbo was awarded the M.B.E. (Member of the Order of the British Empire), one of Britain's highest decorations, for his invaluable service. The Germans were just as satisfied. In June of that year, they had awarded Garbo the Iron Cross. Never before had an agent been decorated by both sides for the same messages.

BIBLIOGRAPHY

CHAPTER 1-"Major Martin Goes to War"

Montagu, Ewen, *Beyond Top Secret Ultra*, Coward, McCann & Geoghegan, New York, 1978.

——, *The Man Who Never Was*, J. B. Lippincott, Philadelphia and New York, 1954.

CHAPTER 2-"The Bombing of America"

Mikesh, Robert C., *Japanese World War II Balloon Bomb Attacks on North America*, Smithsonian Institution, Washington, D.C., 1944.

Webber, Bert, *Retaliation: Japanese Attacks and Allied Countermeasures on the Pacific Coast in World War II*, Oregon State University Press, Corvallis, 1975.

——, "The Bombing of North America," *American History Illustrated*, Gettysburg, Pennsylvania, December 1976.

Wilbur, W. H., "Those Japanese Balloons," *Reader's Digest*, August 1950.

CHAPTER 3-"Operation X-Craft"

Brown, David, *Tirpitz: The Floating Fortress*, United States Naval Institute, Annapolis, Maryland, 1977.

Gallagher, Thomas, *The X-Craft Raid*, Harcourt Brace Jovanovich, New York, 1971.

Kennedy, Ludovic, *The Death of the Tirpitz*, Little, Brown & Co., Boston, 1979.

Peillard, Leonce, *Sink the Tirpitz*, Putnam's, New York, 1968.

CHAPTER 4-"The Battle of the Pips"

Morison, S.E., *History of United States Naval Operations in World War II*, Little Brown & Co., Boston, 1954.

Roscoe, Theodore, *U.S. Destroyer Operations in World War II*, United States Naval Institute, Annapolis, Maryland, 1958.

CHAPTER 5-"The Mafia Connection"

Campbell, Rodney, *The Luciano Project*, McGraw-Hill, New York, 1977.

Gosch, Martin A. and Hammer, Richard, *The Last Testament of Lucky Luciano*, Little Brown & Co., Boston, 1974.

CHAPTER 6-"Indian War Call"

Paul, Doris A., *The Navajo Code Talkers*, Dorrance & Co., Philadelphia, 1973.

Toland, John, *The Rising Sun*, Random House, New York 1970.

Underhill, Ruth, *Here Comes the Navajo*, U.S. Department of the Interior, Haskell Press, New York, 1953.

CHAPTER 7-"Bending the Truth"

Delmer, Sefton, *Black Boomerang*, Viking Press, New York, 1962.

Haldane, R. A., *The Hidden War*, St. Martin's Press, New York, 1978.

Linebarger, Paul, *Psychological Warfare*, Infantry Journal Press, Washington, D.C., 1948.

Seth, Ronald, *The Truth Benders*, L. Frewin, London, 1969.

Thum, Gladys and Thum, Marcella, *The Persuaders: Propaganda in War and Peace*, Atheneum, New York, 1972.

CHAPTER 8-"Go for Broke!"

Fisher, Ernest F., *Cassino to the Alps: United States Army in World War II*, U.S. Government Printing Office, Washington, D.C., 1977.

Murphy, Thomas D., *Ambassadors in Arms*, University of Hawaii Press, Honolulu, 1954.

Nisei in Uniform, U.S. Government Printing Office, Washington, D.C., 1944

CHAPTER 9-"The Big Lie"

Bennett, Ralph, *Ultra in the West: The Normandy Campaign of 1944–1945*, Charles Scribner's Sons, New York, 1980.

Cruikshank, Charles, *Deception in World War II*, Oxford University Press, New York, 1980.

Haldane, R. A., *The Hidden War*, St. Martin's Press, New York, 1978.

Hine, Al, *D-Day: The Invasion of Europe*, American Heritage Publishing Co., New York, 1962.

James, M. E. C., *I Was Monty's Double*, McGraw-Hill, New York, 1954.

Perrault, Gilles, *The Secret of D-Day*, Little, Brown & Co., Boston, 1965.

Ryan, Cornelius, *The Longest Day: June 6, 1944*, Simon & Schuster, New York, 1959.

CHAPTER 10-"V for Vengeance"

Lawson, Don, *The Secret World War II*, Franklin Watts, New York, 1978.

Liddell Hart, Captain B. H., *The German Generals Talk*, William Morrow, New York, 1948.

Lovell, Stanley P., *Of Spies and Stratagems*, Prentice-Hall, Englewood Cliffs, New Jersey, 1963.

CHAPTER 11-"Double Cross"

Hinsley, F. H., *British Intelligence in the Second World War*. Cambridge University Press, New York, 1979.

Masterman, J. C. *The Double Cross System*, Yale University Press, New Haven and London, 1972.

ACKNOWLEDGMENTS

Many people helped in the preparation of this book. Special thanks are offered to Col. Robert N. Waggoner, Chief, Historical Services Division, Department of the Army; Capt. J. L. Schilling, Division of Public Affairs, U.S. Marine Corps; Anna Urband, Office of Information, U.S. Navy; Robert Carlisle, Still Photography, U.S. Navy; J. S. Lucas, Imperial War Museum; Neil Katine, Herb Field Art Studio; Jack D. Carter, Defense Audio Visual Agency; Robert S. Young, U.S. Department of Justice; R. L. Scheina, U.S. Coast Guard; Tom Kawaguchi; Ed Stadnicki; and Bill Sullivan.

126

INDEX